ISBN 0-8373-6670-4

DANTES– **70**

Rudman's Question and Answers on the

DANTES
SUBJECT STANDARDIZED TESTS

Subject Examination In ...

THE CIVIL WAR
AND
RECONSTRUCTION

Questions and Answers

NATIONAL LEARNING CORPORATION
212 MICHAEL DRIVE, SYOSSET, NEW YORK 11791 (516) 921-8888

PASSBOOK®
NOTICE

This book is *SOLELY* intended for, is sold *ONLY* to, and its use is *RESTRICTED* to *individual*, bona fide applicants or candidates who qualify by virtue of having seriously filed applications for appropriate license, certificate, professional and/or promotional advancement, higher school matriculation, scholarship, or other legitimate requirements of educational and/or governmental authorities.

This book is *NOT* intended for use, class instruction, tutoring, training, duplication, copying, reprinting, excerption, or adaptation, etc., by:

(1) Other Publishers

(2) Proprietors and/or Instructors of "Coaching" and/or Preparatory Courses

(3) Personnel and/or Training Divisions of commercial, industrial, and governmental organizations

(4) Schools, colleges, or universities and/or their departments and staffs, including teachers and other personnel

(5) Testing Agencies or Bureaus

(6) Study groups which seek by the purchase of a single volume to copy and/or duplicate and/or adapt this material for use by the group as a whole without having purchased individual volumes for each of the members of the group

(7) Et al.

Such persons would be in violation of appropriate Federal and State statutes.

PROVISION OF LICENSING AGREEMENTS. — Recognized educational commercial, industrial, and governmental institutions and organizations, and others legitimately engaged in educational pursuits, including training, testing, and measurement activities, may address a request for a licensing agreement to the copyright owners, who will determine whether, and under what conditions, including fees and charges, the materials in this book may be used by them. In other words, a licensing facility *exists* for the legitimate use of the material in this book on other than an individual basis. However, it is asseverated and affirmed here that the materials in this book *CANNOT* be used without the receipt of the express permission of such a licensing agreement from the Publishers.

NATIONAL LEARNING CORPORATION
212 Michael Drive
Syosset, New York 11791

Inquiries re licensing agreements should be addressed to:
    The President
    National Learning Corporation
    212 Michael Drive
    Syosset, New York 11791

PASSBOOK SERIES®

THE *PASSBOOK SERIES®* has been created to prepare applicants and candidates for the ultimate academic battlefield – the examination room.

At some time in our lives, each and every one of us may be required to take an examination – for validation, matriculation, admission, qualification, registration, certification, or licensure.

Based on the assumption that every applicant or candidate has met the basic formal educational standards, has taken the required number of courses, and read the necessary texts, the *PASSBOOK SERIES®* furnishes the one special preparation which may assure passing with confidence, instead of failing with insecurity. Examination questions – together with answers – are furnished as the basic vehicle for study so that the mysteries of the examination and its compounding difficulties may be eliminated or diminished by a sure method.

This book is meant to help you pass your examination provided that you qualify and are serious in your objective.

The entire field is reviewed through the huge store of content information which is succinctly presented through a provocative and challenging approach – the question-and-answer method.

A climate of success is established by furnishing the correct answers at the end of each test.

You soon learn to recognize types of questions, forms of questions, and patterns of questioning. You may even begin to anticipate expected outcomes.

You perceive that many questions are repeated or adapted so that you can gain acute insights, which may enable you to score many sure points.

You learn how to confront new questions, or types of questions, and to attack them confidently and work out the correct answers.

You note objectives and emphases, and recognize pitfalls and dangers, so that you may make positive educational adjustments.

Moreover, you are kept fully informed in relation to new concepts, methods, practices, and directions in the field.

You discover that you are actually taking the examination all the time: you are preparing for the examination by "taking" an examination, not by reading extraneous and/or supererogatory textbooks.

In short, this PASSBOOK®, used directedly, should be an important factor in helping you to pass your test.

DANTES Subject Standardized Tests

INTRODUCTION

The DANTES (Defense Activity for Non-Traditional Education Support) subject standardized tests are comprehensive college and graduate level examinations given by the Armed Forces, colleges and graduate schools as end-of-subject course evaluation final examinations or to obtain college equivalency credits in the various subject areas tested.

The DANTES Examination Program enables students to obtain college credit for what they have learned on the job, through self-study, personal interest, correspondence courses or by any other means. It is used by colleges and universities to award college credit to students who demonstrate that they know as much as students completing an equivalent college course. It is a cost-efficient, time-saving way for students to use their knowledge to accomplish their educational goals.

Most schools accept the American Council on Education (ACE) recommendations for the minimum score required and the amount of credit awarded, but not all schools do. Be sure to check the policy regarding the score level required for credit and the number of credits to be awarded.

Not all tests are accepted by all institutions. Even when a test is accepted by an institution, it may not be acceptable for every program at that institution. Before considering testing, ascertain the acceptability of a specific test for a particular course.

Colleges and universities that administer DANTES tests may administer them to any applicant – or they may administer the tests only to students registered at their institution. Decisions about who will be allowed to test are made by the school. Students should contact the test center to determine current policies and schedules for DANTES testing.

Colleges and universities authorized to administer DANTES tests usually do so throughout the calendar year. Each school sets its own fee for test administration and establishes its own testing schedule. Contact the representative at the administering school directly to make arrangements for testing.

Checklist

For Students

✓ Visit **www.getcollegecredit.com** to obtain a list of tests, fact sheets, test preparation materials, participating colleges and universities, and much more.

✓ Contact your school advisor to confirm that the DSST you selected will fit into your curriculum.

✓ Consult the ***DSST Candidate Information Bulletin*** for answers to specific questions.

✓ Contact the test site to schedule your test.

✓ Prepare for your examination by using the fact sheet as a guide.

✓ Take the test.

If you would like a score report sent to your college or university, it is a good idea to bring the four-digit code with you. You must write the DSST Test Center Code for that institution on your answer sheet at the time of testing. DSST Test Center Codes are noted in the DSST Participating Colleges and Universities listing on the Web site.

If you prefer to send a score report to an institution at a later date, there is a transcript fee of $20 for each transcript ordered.

Thomson Prometric
DSST Program
2000 Lenox Drive, Third Floor
Lawrenceville, NJ 08648

Toll-free: 877-471-9860
609-895-5011

E-mail: pnj-dsst@thomson.com

MAKING A COLLEGE DEGREE WITHIN YOUR REACH

Today, there are many educational alternatives to the classroom—you can learn from your job, your reading, your independent study, and special interests you pursue. You may already have learned the subject matter covered by some college-level courses.

The DSST Program is a nationally recognized testing program that gives you the opportunity to receive college credit for learning acquired outside the traditional college classroom. Colleges and universities throughout the United States administer the program, developed by Thomson Prometric, year-round. Annually, over 90,000 DSSTs are administered to individuals who are interested in continuing their education. Take advantage of the DSST testing program; it speeds the educational process and provides the flexibility adults need, making earning a degree more feasible.

Since requirements differ from college to college, please check with the credit-awarding institution before taking a DSST. More than 1,800 colleges and universities currently award credit for DSSTs, and the number is growing every day. You can choose from 37 test titles in the areas of Social Science, Business, Mathematics, Applied Technology, Humanities, and Physical Science. A brief description of each examination is found on the pages that follow.

Reach Your Career Goals Through DSSTs

Use DSSTs to help you earn your degree, get a promotion, or simply demonstrate that you have college-level knowledge in subjects relevant to your work.

Save Time...

You don't have to sit through classes when you have previously acquired the knowledge or experience for most of what is being taught and can learn the rest yourself. You might be able to bypass introductory-level courses in subject areas you already know.

Save Money...

DSSTs save you money because the classes you bypass by earning credit through the DSST Program are classes you won't have to pay for on your way to earning your degree. You can use the money instead to take more advanced courses that can be more challenging and rewarding.

Improve Your Chances for Admission to College

Each college has its own admission policies; however, having passing scores for DSSTs on your transcript can provide strong evidence of how well you can perform at the college level.

Gain Confidence Performing at a College Level

Many adults returning to college find that lack of confidence is often the greatest hurdle to overcome. Passing a DSST demonstrates your ability to perform on a college level.

Make Up for Courses You May Have Missed

You may be ready to graduate from college and find that you are a few credits short of earning your degree. By using semester breaks, vacation time, or leisure time to study independently, you can prepare to take one or more DSSTs, fulfill your academic requirements, and graduate on time.

If You Cannot Attend Regularly Scheduled Classes...

If your lifestyle or responsibilities prevent you from attending regularly scheduled classes, you can earn your college degree from a college offering an external degree program. The DSST Program allows you to earn your degree by study and experience outside the traditional classroom.

Many colleges and universities offer external degree or distance learning programs. For additional information, contact the college you plan to attend or:
Center for Lifelong Learning
American Council on Education
One DuPont Circle NW, Suite 250
Washington, DC 20036
202-939-9475
www.acenet.edu
(Select "Center for Lifelong Learning" under "Programs & Services"
for more information)

Fact Sheets

For each test, there is a Fact Sheet that outlines the topics covered by each test and includes a list of sample questions, a list of recommended references of books that would be useful for review, and the number of credits awarded for a passing score as recommended by the American Council on Education (ACE). *Please note that some schools require scores that are higher than the minimum ACE-recommended passing score.* It is suggested that you check with your college or university to determine what score they require in order to earn credit. You can obtain Fact Sheets by:
- Downloading them from www.getcollegecredit.com
- E-mailing a request to pnj-dsst@thomson.com
- Completing a Candidate Publications Order Form

DSST Online Practice Tests

DSST online practice tests contain items that reflect a *partial range of difficulty* identified in the Content Outline section on each Fact Sheet. There is an online DSST Practice Test in the following categories:
- Mathematics
- Social Science
- Business
- Physical Science
- Applied Technology
- Humanities

Although the online DSST Practice Test questions do not indicate the full range of difficulty you would find in an actual DSST test, they will help you assess your knowledge level. Each online DSST Practice Test can be purchased by visiting www.getcollegecredit.com and clicking on DSST Practice Exams.

TAKING DSST EXAMINATIONS

Earning College Credit for DSST Examinations

To find out if the college of your choice awards credit for passing DSST scores, contact the admissions office or counseling and testing office. The college can also provide information on the scores required for awarding credit, the number of credit hours awarded, and any courses that can be bypassed with satisfactory scores.

It is important that you contact the institution of your choice as early as possible since credit-awarding policies differ among colleges and universities.

Where to Take DSSTs

DSSTs are administered at colleges and universities nationwide. Each location determines the frequency and scheduling of test administrations. To obtain the most current list of participating DSST colleges and universities:

- Visit and download the information from www.getcollegecredit.com
- E-mail pnj-dsst@thomson.com

Scheduling Your Examination

Please be aware that some colleges and universities provide DSST testing services to enrolled students only. After you have selected a college or university that administers DSSTs, you will need to contact them to schedule your test date.

The fee to take a DSST is $60 per test. This fee entitles you to two score reports after the test is scored. One will be sent directly to you and the other will be sent to the college or university that you designate on your answer sheet. You may pay the test fee with a certified check or U.S. money order made payable to Thomson Prometric or you may charge the test fee to your Visa, MasterCard or American Express credit card. Note: The credit card statement will reflect a charge from Thomson Prometric for all DSST examinations. _(Declined credit card charges will be assessed an additional $25 processing fee.)_

In addition, the test site may also require a test administration fee for each examination, to be paid directly to the institution. Contact the test site to determine its administration fee and payment policy.

Other Testing Arrangements

If you are unable to find a participating DSST college or university in your area, you may want to contact the testing office of a local accredited college or university to determine whether a representative from that office will agree to administer the test(s) for you.

The school's representative should then contact the DSST Program at 866-794-3497 to arrange for this administration. If you are unable to locate a test site, contact Thomson Prometric for assistance at pnj-dsst@thomson.com or 866-794-3497.

Testing Accommodations for Students with Disabilities

Thomson Prometric is committed to serving test takers with disabilities by providing services and reasonable testing accommodations as set forth in the provisions of the _Americans with Disabilities Act_ (ADA). If you have a disability, as prescribed by the ADA, and require special testing services or arrangements, please contact the test administrator at the test site. You will be asked to submit to the test administrator documentation of your disability and your request for special accommodations. The test administrator will then forward your documentation along with your request for testing accommodations to Thomson Prometric for approval.

Please submit your request as far in advance of your test date as possible so that the necessary accommodations can be made. Only test takers with documented disabilities are eligible for special accommodations.

On the Day of the Examination

It is important to review this information and to have the correct identification present on the day of the examination:

- Arrive on time as a courtesy to the test administrator.
- Bring a valid form of government-issued identification that includes a current photo and your signature (acceptable documents include a driver's license, passport, state-issued identification card or military identification). *Anyone who fails to present valid identification will not be allowed to test.*
- Bring several No. 2 (soft-lead) sharpened pencils with good erasers, a watch, and a black pen if you will be writing an essay.
- Do not bring books or papers.
- Do not bring an alarm watch that beeps, a telephone, or a phone beeper into the testing room.
- The use of nonprogrammable calculators, slide rules, scratch paper and/or other materials is permitted for some of the tests.

DSST SCORING POLICIES

Your DSST examination scores are reported only to you, unless you request that they be sent elsewhere. If you want your scores sent to your college, you must provide the correct DSST code number of the school on your answer sheet at the time you take the test. See the *DSST Directory of Colleges and Universities* on the Web site www.getcollegecredit.com.

If your institution is not listed, contact Thomson Prometric at 866-794-3497 to establish a code number. (Some schools may require a student to be enrolled prior to receiving a score report.)

Receiving Your Score Report

Allow approximately four weeks after testing to receive your score report.

Calling DSST Customer Service before the required four-week score processing time has elapsed will not expedite the processing of your scores. Due to privacy and security requirements, scores will not be reported to students over the telephone under any circumstance.

Scoring of Principles of Public Speaking Speeches

The speech portion of the *Principles of Public Speaking* examination will be sent to speech raters who are faculty members at accredited colleges that currently teach or have previously taught the course. Scores for the *Principles of Public Speaking* examination are available six to eight weeks from receipt by Thomson Prometric. If you take the *Principles of Public Speaking* examination and fail (either the objective, speech portion, or both), you must follow the retesting policy waiting period of six months (180 days) before retaking the entire exam.

Essays

The essays for *Ethics in America* and *Technical Writing* are <u>optional</u> and thus are not scored by raters. The essays are forwarded to the college or university that you designate, along with your score report, for their use in determining the award of credit. <u>Before taking the *Ethics in America* or *Technical Writing* examinations, check with your college or university to determine whether the essay is required.</u>

NOTE: *Principles of Public Speaking* speech topic cassette tapes and essays are kept on file at Thomson Prometric for one year from the date of administration.

How to Get Transcripts

There is a $20 fee for each transcript you request. Payment must be in the form of a certified check, U.S. money order payable to Thomson Prometric, or credit card. Personal checks and debit cards are NOT an acceptable method of payment. One transcript may include scores for one or more examinations taken. To request a transcript, download the Transcript Order Form from www.getcollegecredit.com.

DESCRIPTION OF THE DSST EXAMINATIONS

Mathematics

• **Fundamentals of College Algebra** covers mathematical concepts such as fundamental algebraic operations; linear, absolute value; quadratic equations, inequalities, radials, exponents and logarithms, factoring polynomials and graphing. The use of a nonprogrammable, handheld calculator is permitted.

• **Principles of Statistics** tests the understanding of the various topics of statistics, both qualitatively and quantitatively, and the ability to apply statistical methods to solve a variety of problems. The topics included in this test are descriptive statistics; correlation and regression; probability; chance models and sampling and tests of significance. The use of a nonprogrammable, handheld calculator is permitted.

Social Science

• **Art of the Western World** deals with the history of art during the following periods: classical; Romanesque and Gothic; early Renaissance; high Renaissance, Baroque; rococo; neoclassicism and romanticism; realism, impressionism and post-impressionism; early twentieth century; and post-World War II.

• **Western Europe Since 1945** tests the knowledge of basic facts and terms and the understanding of concepts and principles related to the areas of the historical background of the aftermath of the Second World War and rebuilding of Europe; national political systems; issues and policies in Western European societies; European institutions and processes; and Europe's relations with the rest of the world.

• **An Introduction to the Modern Middle East** emphasizes core knowledge (including geography, Judaism, Christianity, Islam, ethnicity); nineteenth-century European impact; twentieth-century Western influences; World Wars I and II; new nations; social and cultural changes (1900-1960) and the Middle East from 1960 to present.

• **Human/Cultural Geography** includes the Earth and basic facts (coordinate systems, maps, physiography, atmosphere, soils and vegetation, water); culture and environment, spatial processes (social processes, modern economic systems, settlement patterns, political geography); and regional geography.

• **Rise and Fall of the Soviet Union** covers Russia under the Old Regime; the Revolutionary Period; New Economic Policy; Pre-war Stalinism; The Second World War; Post-war Stalinism; The Khrushchev Years; The Brezhnev Era; and reform and collapse.

• **A History of the Vietnam War** covers the history of the roots of the Vietnam War; the First Vietnam War (1946-1954); pre-war developments (1954-1963); American involvement in the Vietnam War; Tet (1968); Vietnamizing the War (1968-1973); Cambodia and Laos; peace; legacies and lessons.

• **The Civil War and Reconstruction** covers the Civil War from presecession (1861) through Reconstruction. It includes causes of the war; secession; Fort Sumter; the war in the east and in the west; major battles; the political situation; assassination of Lincoln; end of the Confederacy; and Reconstruction.

• **Foundations of Education** includes topics such as contemporary issues in education; past and current influences on education (philosophies, democratic ideals, social/economic influences); and the interrelationships between contemporary issues and influences.

• **Life-span Developmental Psychology** covers models and theories; methods of study; ethical issues; biological development; perception, learning and memory; cognition and language; social, emotional, and personality development; social behaviors, family life cycle, extrafamilial settings; singlehood and cohabitation; occupational development and retirement; adjustment to life stresses; and bereavement and loss.

• **Drug and Alcohol Abuse** includes such topics as drug use in society; classification of drugs; pharmacological principles; alcohol (types, effects of, alcoholism); general principles and use of sedative hypnotics, narcotic analgesics, stimulants, and hallucinogens; other drugs (inhalants, steroids); and prevention/treatment.

• **General Anthropology** deals with anthropology as a discipline; theoretical perspectives; physical anthropology; archaeology; social organization; economic organization; political organization; religion; and modernization and application of anthropology.

• **Introduction to Law Enforcement** includes topics such as history and professional movement of law enforcement; overview of the U.S. criminal justice system; police systems in the U.S.; police organization, management, and issues; and U.S. law and precedents.

• **Criminal Justice** deals with criminal behavior (crime in the U.S., theories of crime, types of crime); the criminal justice system (historical origins, legal foundations, due process); police; the court system (history and organization, adult court system, juvenile court, pre-trial and post-trial processes); and corrections.

• **Fundamentals of Counseling** covers historical development (significant influences and people); counselor roles and functions; the counseling relationship; and theoretical approaches to counseling.

Business
• **Principles of Finance** deals with financial statements and planning; time value of money; working capital management; valuation and characteristics; capital budgeting; cost of capital; risk and return; and international financial management. The use of a nonprogrammable, handheld calculator is permitted.

• **Principles of Financial Accounting** includes topics such as general concepts and principles, accounting cycle and classification; transaction analysis; accruals and deferrals; cash and internal control; current accounts; long- and short-term liabilities; capital stock; and financial statements. The use of a nonprogrammable, handheld calculator is permitted.

• **Human Resource Management** covers general employment issues; job analysis; training and development; performance appraisals; compensation issues; security issues; personnel legislation and regulation; labor relations and current issues; an overview of the Human Resource Management Field; Human Resource Planning; Staffing; training and development; compensation issues; safety and health; employee rights and discipline; employment law; labor relations and current issues and trends.

• **Organizational Behavior** deals with the study of organizational behavior (scientific approaches, research designs, data collection methods); individual processes and characteristics; interpersonal and group processes and characteristics; organizational processes and characteristics; and change and development processes.

• **Principles of Supervision** deals with the roles and responsibilities of the supervisor; management functions (planning, organization and staffing, directing at the supervisory level); and other topics (legal issues, stress management, union environments, quality concerns).

• **Business Law II** covers topics such as sales of goods; debtor and creditor relations; business organizations; property; and commercial paper.

• **Introduction to Computing** includes topics such as history and technological generations; hardware/software; applications to information technology; program development; data management; communications and connectivity; and computing and society. The use of a nonprogrammable, handheld calculator is permitted.

• **Management Information Systems** covers systems theory, analysis and design of systems, hardware and software; database management; telecommunications; management of the MIS functional area and informational support.

• **Introduction to Business** deals with economic issues affecting business; international business; government and business; forms of business ownership; small business, entrepreneurship and franchise; management process; human resource management; production and operations; marketing management; financial management; risk management and insurance; and management and information systems.

• **Money and Banking** covers the role and kinds of money; commercial banks and other financial intermediaries; central banking and the Federal Reserve system; money and macroeconomics activity; monetary policy in the U.S.; and the international monetary system.

• **Personal Finance** includes topics such as financial goals and values; budgeting; credit and debt; major purchases; taxes; insurance; investments; and retirement and estate planning. The use of auxiliary materials, such as calculators and slide rules, is NOT permitted.

• **Business Mathematics** deals with basic operations with integers, fractions, and decimals; round numbers; ratios; averages; business graphs; simple interest; compound interest and annuities; net pay and deductions; discounts and markups; depreciation and net worth; corporate securities; distribution of ownership; and stock and asset turnover.

Physical Science

• **Astronomy** covers the history of astronomy, celestial mechanics; celestial systems; astronomical instruments; the solar system; nature and evolution; the galaxy; the universe; determining astronomical distances; and life in the universe.

• **Here's to Your Health** covers mental health and behavior; human development and relationships; substance abuse; fitness and nutrition; risk factors, disease, and disease prevention; and safety, consumer awareness, and environmental concerns.

• **Environment and Humanity** deals with topics such as ecological concepts (ecosystems, global ecology, food chains and webs); environmental impacts; environmental management and conservation; and political processes and the future.

• **Principles of Physical Science I** includes physics: Newton's Laws of Motion; energy and momentum; thermodynamics; wave and optics; electricity and magnetism; chemistry: properties of matter; atomic theory and structure; and chemical reactions.

• **Physical Geology** covers Earth materials; igneous, sedimentary, and metamorphic rocks; surface processes (weathering, groundwater, glaciers, oceanic systems, deserts and winds, hydrologic cycle); internal Earth processes; and applications (mineral and energy resources, environmental geology).

Applied Technology

• **Technical Writing** covers topics such as theory and practice of technical writing; purpose, content, and organizational patterns of common types of technical documents; elements of various technical reports; and technical editing. Students have the option to write a short essay on one of the technical topics provided. Thomson Prometric will not score the essay; however, for determining the award of credit, a copy of the essay will be forwarded to the college or university you've designated along with the score report or transcript.

Humanities

• **Ethics in America** deals with ethical traditions (Greek views, Biblical traditions, moral law, consequential ethics, feminist ethics); ethical analysis of issues arising in interpersonal and personal-societal relationships and in professional and occupational roles; and relationships between ethical traditions and the ethical analysis of situations. Students have the option to write an essay to analyze a morally problematic situation in terms of issues relevant to a decision and arguments for alternative positions. Thomson Prometric will not score the essay; however, for determining the award of credit, a copy of the essay will be forwarded to the college or university you've designated along with the score report or transcript.

• **Introduction to World Religions** covers topics such as dimensions and approaches to religion; primal religions; Hinduism; Buddhism; Confucianism; Taoism; Judaism; Christianity; and Islam.

• **Principles of Public Speaking** consists of two parts: Part One consists of multiple-choice questions covering considerations of Principles of Public Speaking; audience analysis; purposes of speeches; structure/organization; content/supporting materials; research; language and style; delivery; communication apprehension; listening and feedback; and criticism and evaluation. Part Two requires the student to record an impromptu persuasive speech that will be scored.

FREQUENTLY ASKED QUESTIONS ABOUT DSSTs

In order to pass the test, must I study from one of the recommended references?

The recommended references are a listing of books that were being used as textbooks in college courses of the same or similar title at the time the test was developed. Appropriate textbooks for study are not limited to those listed in the fact sheet. If you wish to obtain study resources to prepare for the examination, you may reference either the current edition of the listed titles or textbooks currently used at a local college or university for the same class title. It is recommended that you reference more than one textbook on the topics outlined in the fact sheet. You should begin by checking textbook content against the content outline included on the front page of the DSST fact sheet before selecting textbooks that cover the text content from which to study. Textbooks may be found at the campus bookstore of a local college or university offering a course on the subject.

Is there a penalty for guessing on the tests?

There is no penalty for guessing on DSSTs, so you should mark an answer for each question.

How much time will I have to complete the test?

Many DSSTs can be completed within 90 minutes; however, additional time can be allowed if necessary.

What should I do if I find a test question irregularity?

Continue testing and then report the irregularity to the test administrator after the test. This may be done by asking that the test administrator note the irregularity on the Supervisor's Irregularity Report or you can write to Thomson Prometric, DSST Program, 2000 Lenox Drive, Third Floor, Lawrenceville, NJ 08648, and indicate the form and question number(s) or circumstances as well as your name and address.

When will I receive my score report?

Allow approximately four weeks from the date of testing to receive your score report. Allow six to eight weeks to receive a score report for the *Principles of Public Speaking* examination.

Will my test scores be released without my permission?

Your test score will not be released to anyone other than the school you designate on your answer sheet unless you write to us and ask us to send a transcript elsewhere. Instructions about how to do this can be found on your score report. Your scores may be used for research purposes, but individual scores are never made public nor are individuals identified if research findings are made public.

If I do not achieve a passing score on the test, how long must I wait until I can take the test again?

If you do not receive a score on the test that will enable you to obtain credit for the course, you may take the test again after six months (180 days). Please do not attempt to take the test before six months (180 days) have passed because you will receive a score report marked *invalid* and your test fee will not be refunded.

Can my test scores be canceled?

The test administrator is required to report any irregularities to Thomson Prometric. The consequence of bringing unauthorized materials into the testing room, or giving or receiving help, will be the forfeiture of your test fee and the invalidation of test scores. The DSST Program reserves the right to cancel scores and not issue score reports in such situations.

What can I do if I feel that my test scores were not accurately reported?

Thomson Prometric recognizes the extreme importance of test results to candidates and has a multi-step quality-control procedure to help ensure that reported scores are accurate. If you have reason to believe that your score(s) were not accurately reported, you may request to have your answer sheet reviewed and hand scored.

The fees for this service are:
• $20 fee if requested within six months of the test date
• $30 fee if requested more than six months from the test date
• $30 fee if a re-evaluation of the *Principles of Public Speaking* speech is requested

The fee for this service can be paid by credit card or by certified check or U.S. money order payable to Thomson Prometric. Submit your request for score verification along with the appropriate fee or credit card information (credit card number and expiration date) to Thomson Prometric, DSST Program, 2000 Lenox Drive, Third Floor, Lawrenceville, NJ 08648. Include your full name, the test title, the date you took the test, and your Social Security number. Candidates will be notified if a scoring discrepancy is discovered within four weeks of receipt of the request.

What does ACE recommendation mean?

The ACE recommendation is the minimum passing score recommended by the American Council on Education for any given test. It is equivalent to the average score of students in the DSST norming sample who received a grade of C for the course. Some schools require a score higher than the ACE recommendation.

Who is NLC?

National Learning Corporation (NLC) has been successfully preparing candidates for 40 years for over 5,000 exams. NLC publishes Passbook® study guides to help candidates prepare for all DANTES and CLEP exams and almost every other type of exam from high school through adult career.

Go to our website — www.passbooks.com — or call (800) 632-8888 for information about ordering our Passbooks.

To get detailed information on the DSST program and DSST preparation materials, visit www.getcollegecredit.com.

If you are interested in taking the DSST exams, call 877-471-9860 or e-mail pnj-dsst@thomson.com.

Fact Sheet

DANTES Subject Standardized Tests

THE CIVIL WAR AND RECONSTRUCTION

TEST INFORMATION

This test was developed to enable schools to award credit to students for knowledge equivalent to that which is learned by students taking the course. The school may choose to award college credit to the student based on the achievement of a passing score. The passing score for each examination is determined by the school based on recommendations from the American Council on Education (ACE). This minimum credit-awarding score is equal to the mean score of students in the norming sample who received a grade of C in the course. Some schools set their own standards for awarding credit and may require a higher score than the ACE recommendation. Students should obtain this information from the institution where they expect to receive credit.

CONTENT

The following topics, which are commonly taught in courses on this subject, are covered by this examination.

Approximate Percent

I. Causes of the War   11%
  A. United States society in the mid-nineteenth century
    1. Industrialization
    2. Immigration
    3. Religiosity
    4. Standard of living
    5. Demographics
  B. Growing differences between the North and South

Approximate Percent

  C. Slavery as a Southern institution
    1. Importance of cotton
    2. Living conditions of slaves
  D. Abolition movement
    1. Leaders
    2. Methods and tactics
    3. *Uncle Tom's Cabin*
  E. Westward expansion of Free and Slave territory
    1. Missouri Compromise
    2. Mexican War
    3. Compromise of 1850
    4. Kansas - Nebraska Act
    5. Birth of Republican party
    6. Kansas wars
    7. Dred Scott decision
  F. John Brown's raid on Harper's Ferry
  G. Political situation in 1860
    1. Split in Democratic party
    2. Republican party
    3. Abraham Lincoln
    4. Election results

II. 1861   11%
  A. Secession
    1. South Carolina's role
    2. Border states
    3. Government of Confederation
  B. Fort Sumter
  C. Union Army *v.* Confederate Army
    1. Leadership
    2. Preparedness
    3. Volunteers
  D. First Manassas (Bull Run)

from the official announcement for instructional purposes

 A subsidiary of

III. 1862   **22%**
  A. Political situation -
     North and South
     1. Lincoln's cabinet
     2. Davis's cabinet
        Divisiveness in
        the South
        a. Conscription
        b. States rights
     3. Southern hope of
        European aid
  B. Army of Potomac under
     McClellan
  C. War in the West
     1. North's plan to
        control Mississippi
     2. Generals Grant, Buell
        and Sherman
  D. War in the East
     1. Peninsular campaign
     2. Naval involvement
        a. Blockade and
           blockade runners
        b. *Monitor v. Merrimac*
     3. Generals Lee and
        Jackson
  E. Major battles
     1. Shiloh
     2. Second Manassas
     3. Antietam
     4. Fredericksburg
  F. Emancipation
     Proclamation

IV. 1863   **21%**
  A. Casualties
     1. Causes of casualties
     2. Care of wounded
        and sick
     3. Prisoners of war
  B. Role of women in the war,
     North and South
  C. Black Americans and
     the war
     1. Free Black volunteers
     2. Slaves in the South
     3. Runaway slaves

  D. Political situation
     1. North
        a. Conscription
        b. Copperheads
        c. Anti-emancipation
           sentiment
        d. Profiteering
     2. South
        a. Inadequate central
           government
        b. Inflation
        c. Shortages
  E. Major battles
     1. Chancellorsville
     2. Chicamauga
     3. Chattanooga
     4. Stones River
        (Murfreesboro)
     5. Vicksburg
     6. Gettysburg

V. 1864 to May 1865   **22%**
  A. Political situation
     1. Northern demoralization
     2. Presidential election
        in North
     3. South cut in half and
        isolated
  B. War in the West
     1. Sherman's march
        through Georgia
     2. Generals Johnston
        and Forrest
     3. Major battles
        a. Atlanta
        b. Mobile Bay
  C. War in the East
     1. Grant and the Army of
        the Potomac
     2. Lee and the Army of
        Northern Virginia
     3. Major battles
        a. Wilderness
        b. Spotsylvania
        c. Cold Harbor
        d. Shenandoah Valley
           campaign
        e. Petersburg

D. Sherman's continued
march through the South
   1. Destruction of South's
      civilian base
   2. Logistics
E. Fall of Richmond, flight
   of Confederate government
F. Lee's surrender
G. Assassination of Lincoln
H. End of the Confederacy
   1. Johnston's surrender
   2. Davis's capture
I. Cost of the War
   1. Human
   2. Economic
   3. Cultural

VI. Reconstruction   **13%**
   A. Presidential reconstruction
      plans
      1. Lincoln
      2. Johnson
   B. Congressional reconstruction
      plans
      1. Radical Republicans
      2. Reconstruction Acts
      3. Fourteenth and
         Fifteenth Amendments
      4. Impeachment
      5. Freedmen's Bureau
      6. Civil Rights Act
   C. Reconstruction in the South
      1. Response to Johnson's
         policies
      2. Elected Black office-
         holders
      3. Scalawags and carpet-
         baggers
      4. Secret terrorist societies
   D. End of Reconstruction
      1. Restoration of White
         government
      2. Election of 1876
      3. Compromise of 1877

Questions on the test require candidates to
demonstrate the following abilities.

- Knowledge of basic facts and terms
  (about 100% of the examination)

SAMPLE QUESTIONS

1. Which of the following correctly states a major
   difference between the population of the North
   and South at the middle of the nineteenth
   century?

   (A) In the North, the vast majority of the adult
       White population was literate, while in the
       South less than half the adult White
       population could read and write.
   (B) In the South, people were much more
       religious than people in the North,
       attended church more frequently, and
       often participated in religious
       reawakenings.
   (C) In the North, the White population included
       large numbers of immigrants, while in the
       south the White population was largely of
       British descent.
   (D) In the South, a larger proportion of the
       White population had traveled extensively
       within the region, while the Northern
       White population remained familiar only
       with the area in which they were born.

2. Prior to his attack on Harper's Ferry, John
   Brown was a

   (A) free-state agitator in Kansas
   (B) publisher of a leading abolitionist newspaper
   (C) slave owner in Missouri
   (D) station owner on the Underground Railroad

3. When the Southern states began to secede, Kentucky's response was

(A) enthusiastic support for the South, followed by Kentucky's secession
(B) reluctant support for the South, followed by Kentucky's secession
(C) a declaration of neutrality, followed by a gradual shift to Unionism
(D) a firm resolve to remain in the Union, followed by an enthusiastic response to Lincoln's call for troops

4. Through the course of the Civil War, which of the following was true of Jefferson Davis's cabinet?

(A) It remained stable in makeup and firm in support of the president.
(B) It remained stable in makeup but opposed to the president on many issues.
(C) Its members changed considerably but remained constant in support for the president.
(D) Its members changed considerably and were divided in their support for the president.

5. The South's naval strategy was to use its

(A) large navy to attack Northern ports and bring the war to the North
(B) large navy to defend its ports and prevent a Union blockade
(C) relatively small navy to protect its ports and keep them open for blockade runners
(D) relatively small navy to convoy supply ships from Europe and South America

6. Of those who died as a result of the war, the majority were

(A) civilians deliberately or accidentally killed by hostile troops
(B) soldiers killed outright in combat
(C) soldiers who died later of wounds received in battle
(D) soldiers who died of disease

7. The last major Confederate stronghold on the Mississippi River was

(A) Memphis
(B) Vicksburg
(C) New Orleans
(D) Fort Donelson

8. Which of the following nearly caused the outbreak of hostilities between the United States and Great Britain?

(A) Britain's willingness to receive the Confederate cruiser *Alabama* in its ports
(B) British gunrunning to the Confederate states through the Union blockade
(C) British reactions to Lincoln's Emancipation Proclamation
(D) British objections to the seizure of two Confederate diplomats traveling on a British ship

9. Which of the following is a true statement about the Union presidential election of 1864?

(A) It was the first presidential election ever held by a nation involved in a civil war.
(B) It attracted little public interest because the people of the North were occupied with the war effort.
(C) Lincoln's reelection was considered a certainty because the nation did not want to change governments in the middle of the war.
(D) Lincoln's reelection was considered unlikely because Lincoln had failed to support abolition prior to the war.

10. The Union general in command of the Shenandoah Valley campaigns of 1864 was

(A) Philip Kearny
(B) Philip Sheridan
(C) William T. Sherman
(D) George A. Custer

11. Grant's confrontation with Lee at Petersburg can best be described as a

(A) Confederate rout of the Union army
(B) swift, decisive victory for the Union army
(C) tragic blunder on the part of the Union high command
(D) prolonged siege ending in Union victory

12. Under the Fourteenth Amendment, many of those who had served in the Confederate government or army were

(A) automatically reinstated as full citizens of the United States
(B) forbidden to bear arms
(C) forbidden to hold public office
(D) interned for a minimum of six months

STUDYING FOR THE EXAMINATION

The following is a list of reference publications that were being used as textbooks in college courses of the same or similar title at the time the test was developed. Appropriate textbooks for study are not limited to those listed below. If you wish to obtain study resources to prepare for the examination, you may reference either the current edition of the following titles **or** textbooks currently used at a local college or university for the same class title. It is recommended that you reference **more than one textbook** on the topics outlined in this fact sheet. You should **begin by checking textbook content against the content outline** included on the front page of this Fact Sheet **before** selecting textbooks that cover the test content from which to study. Textbooks may be found at the campus bookstore of a local college or university offering a course on the subject.

Sources for study material suggested but not limited to the following:

Boatner, Mark Mayo. *The Civil War Dictionary*. Rev. ed. New York, NY: David McKay, current edition.

Boritt, Gabor S. ed. *Why the Confederacy Lost*. New York, NY: Oxford University Press, current edition.

Burns, Ken and Burns, Ric. *The Civil War*. Florentine Films, PBS Video, Alexandria, VA, current edition.

Donald, David. ed. *Why the North Won the Civil War*. New York, NY: Macmillan, current edition.

Eaton, Clement. *A History of the Southern Confederacy*. New York, NY: The Free Press, current edition.

Foner, Eric. *Reconstruction: America's Unfinished Revolution*. New York, NY: Harper and Row, current edition.

Foote, Shelby. *The Civil War, A Narrative*. 3 vols. New York, NY: Random House, current edition.

McPherson, James. *Battle Cry of Freedom: The Civil War Era*. New York, NY: Oxford University Press, current edition.

McPherson, James. *Ordeal by Fire: The Civil War and Reconstruction*. New York, NY: McGraw-Hill, current edition.

Nevins, Allan. *War for the Union*. 4 vols. New York, NY: Charles Scribner's Sons, current edition.

Nolan, Alan T. *Lee Considered: General Robert E. Lee and Civil War History*. Chapel Hill: University of North Carolina Press, current edition.

Paludan, Phillip Shaw. *A People's Contest: The Union and Civil War*. New York, NY: Harper and Row, current edition.

Randall, J.G. and Donald, David. *The Civil War and Reconstruction*. Lexington, MA: D.C. Heath and Co., current edition.

Thomas, Benjamin P. *Abraham Lincoln: A Biography*. New York, NY: Modern Library, current edition.

Thomas, Emory M. *The Confederate Nation*. New York, NY: Harper and Row, current edition.

Current textbook used by a local college or university for a course on the subject.

CREDIT RECOMMENDATIONS

The Center for Adult Learning and Educational Credentials of the American Council on Education (ACE) has reviewed and evaluated the DSST examination development process. The American Council on Education has made the following recommendations:

Area or Course
  Equivalent: The Civil War &
                             Reconstruction
Level: Upper-level baccalaureate
Amount of Credit: Three (3) semester hours
Source: ACE Commission on
                               Educational Credit
                               and Credentials

INFORMATION

Colleges and universities that would like additional information about the national norming, or assistance in local norming or score validation studies should write to: DSST Program, Mail Stop 11-P, The Chauncey Group International, 664 Rosedale Road, Princeton, New Jersey 08540.

It is advisable that schools develop a consistent policy about awarding credit based on scores from this test and that the policy be reviewed periodically. The Chauncey Group will be happy to help schools in this effort.

HOW TO TAKE A TEST

You have studied long, hard and conscientiously.

With your official admission card in hand, and your heart pounding, you have been admitted to the examination room.

You note that there are several hundred other applicants in the examination room waiting to take the same test.

They all appear to be equally well prepared.

You know that nothing but your best effort will suffice. The "moment of truth" is at hand: you now have to demonstrate objectively, in writing, your knowledge of content and your understanding of subject matter.

You are fighting the most important battle of your life—to pass and/or score high on an examination which will determine your career and provide the economic basis for your livelihood.

What extra, special things should you know and should you do in taking the examination?

BEFORE THE TEST

YOUR PHYSICAL CONDITION IS IMPORTANT
    If you are not well, you can't do your best work on tests. If you are half asleep, you can't do your best either. Here are some tips:

1) Get about the same amount of sleep you usually get. Don't stay up all night before the test, either partying or worrying—DON'T DO IT!
2) If you wear glasses, be sure to wear them when you go to take the test. This goes for hearing aids, too.
3) If you have any physical problems that may keep you from doing your best, be sure to tell the person giving the test. If you are sick or in poor health, you really cannot do your best on any test. You can always come back and take the test some other time.

AT THE TEST

EXAMINATION TECHNIQUES
1) Read the general instructions carefully. These are usually printed on the first page of the exam booklet. As a rule, these instructions refer to the timing of the examination; the fact that you should not start work until the signal and must stop work at a signal, etc. If there are any *special* instructions, such as a choice of questions to be answered, make sure that you note this instruction carefully.

2) When you are ready to start work on the examination, that is as soon as the signal has been given, read the instructions to each question booklet, underline any key words or phrases, such as *least, best, outline, describe* and the like. In this way you will tend to answer as requested rather than discover on reviewing your paper that you *listed without describing*, that you selected the *worst* choice rather than the *best* choice, etc.

3) If the examination is of the objective or multiple-choice type – that is, each question will also give a series of possible answers: A, B, C or D, and you are called upon to select the best answer and write the letter next to that answer on your answer paper – it is advisable to start answering each question in turn. There may be anywhere from 50 to 100 such questions in the three or four hours allotted and you can see how much time would be taken if you read through all the questions before beginning to answer any. Furthermore, if you come across a question or group of questions which you know would be difficult to answer, it would undoubtedly affect your handling of all the other questions.

4) If the examination is of the essay type and contains but a few questions, it is a moot point as to whether you should read all the questions before starting to answer any one. Of course, if you are given a choice – say five out of seven and the like – then it is essential to read all the questions so you can eliminate the two which are most difficult. If, however, you are asked to answer all the questions, there may be danger in trying to answer the easiest one first because you may find that you will spend too much time on it. The best technique is to answer the first question, then proceed to the second, etc.

5) Time your answers. Before the exam begins, write down the time it started, then add the time allowed for the examination and write down the time it must be completed, then divide the time available somewhat as follows:
   - If 3-1/2 hours are allowed, that would be 210 minutes. If you have 80 objective-type questions, that would be an average of 2-1/2 minutes per question. Allow yourself no more than 2 minutes per question, or a total of 160 minutes, which will permit about 50 minutes to review.
   - If for the time allotment of 210 minutes there are 7 essay questions to answer, that would average about 30 minutes a question. Give yourself only 25 minutes per question so that you have about 35 minutes to review.

6) The most important instruction is to *read each question* and make sure you know what is wanted. The second most important instruction is to *time yourself properly* so that you answer every question. The third most important instruction is to *answer every question*. Guess if you have to but include something for each question. Remember that you will receive no credit for a blank and will probably receive some credit if you write something in answer to an essay question. If you guess a letter – say "B" for a multiple-choice question – you may have guessed right. If you leave a blank as an answer to a multiple-choice question, the examiners may respect your

feelings but it will not add a point to your score. Some exams may penalize you for wrong answers, so in such cases *only*, you may not want to guess unless you have some basis for your answer.

7) Suggestions
   a. Objective-type questions
      1. Examine the question booklet for proper sequence of pages and questions
      2. Read all instructions carefully
      3. Skip any question which seems too difficult; return to it after all other questions have been answered
      4. Apportion your time properly; do not spend too much time on any single question or group of questions
      5. Note and underline key words – *all, most, fewest, least, best, worst, same, opposite*, etc.
      6. Pay particular attention to negatives
      7. Note unusual option, e.g., unduly long, short, complex, different or similar in content to the body of the question
      8. Observe the use of "hedging" words – *probably, may, most likely*, etc.
      9. Make sure that your answer is put next to the same number as the question
      10. Do not second-guess unless you have good reason to believe the second answer is definitely more correct
      11. Cross out original answer if you decide another answer is more accurate; do not erase until you are ready to hand your paper in
      12. Answer all questions; guess unless instructed otherwise
      13. Leave time for review

   b. Essay questions
      1. Read each question carefully
      2. Determine exactly what is wanted. Underline key words or phrases.
      3. Decide on outline or paragraph answer
      4. Include many different points and elements unless asked to develop any one or two points or elements
      5. Show impartiality by giving pros and cons unless directed to select one side only
      6. Make and write down any assumptions you find necessary to answer the questions
      7. Watch your English, grammar, punctuation and choice of words
      8. Time your answers; don't crowd material

8) Answering the essay question

Most essay questions can be answered by framing the specific response around several key words or ideas. Here are a few such key words or ideas:

M's: manpower, materials, methods, money, management
P's: purpose, program, policy, plan, procedure, practice, problems, pitfalls, personnel, public relations

a. Six basic steps in handling problems:
   1. Preliminary plan and background development
   2. Collect information, data and facts
   3. Analyze and interpret information, data and facts
   4. Analyze and develop solutions as well as make recommendations
   5. Prepare report and sell recommendations
   6. Install recommendations and follow up effectiveness

b. Pitfalls to avoid
   1. *Taking things for granted* – A statement of the situation does not necessarily imply that each of the elements is necessarily true; for example, a complaint may be invalid and biased so that all that can be taken for granted is that a complaint has been registered
   2. *Considering only one side of a situation* – Wherever possible, indicate several alternatives and then point out the reasons you selected the best one
   3. *Failing to indicate follow up* – Whenever your answer indicates action on your part, make certain that you will take proper follow-up action to see how successful your recommendations, procedures or actions turn out to be
   4. *Taking too long in answering any single question* – Remember to time your answers properly

EXAMINATION SECTION

EXAMINATION SECTION
TEST 1

DIRECTIONS: Each question or incomplete statement is followed by several suggested answers or completions. Select the one that BEST answers the question or completes the statement. *PRINT THE LETTER OF THE CORRECT ANSWER IN THE SPACE AT THE RIGHT.*

1. Which of the following Midwestern states was considered to be the heart of *Copperhead country* during the latter years of the Civil War?
   A. Missouri
   B. Ohio
   C. Minnesota
   D. Iowa

1.___

2. Throughout the War, the Cabinet members with whom President Lincoln worked most closely were
   A. Edward Bates and Edwin M. Stanton
   B. Edwin M. Stanton and William H. Seward
   C. Gideon Welles and Simon Cameron
   D. William H. Seward and Salmon P. Chase

2.___

3. Each of the following was an element of the Wade-Davis reconstruction bill passed by the Republicans in 1864 EXCEPT
   A. restoration to the Union contingent upon an oath of allegiance from 50 percent of voters in a state
   B. permission of suffrage for all whites who took an oath of future loyalty
   C. the mandated election of delegates to a constitutional convention
   D. specific legal safeguards for the liberty of freedmen

3.___

4. Which of the following was NOT a *border* state during the Civil War conflict?
   A. Virginia   B. Missouri   C. Maryland   D. Kentucky

4.___

5. Which of the following was not a significant problem associated with the practice of *paroling* prisoners of war during the Civil War?
   A. Paroled prisoners expected to be sent home.
   B. Most paroled prisoners would simply return to active duty.
   C. Order in parole camps was difficult to maintain.
   D. It encouraged some soldiers to fall into the hands of the enemy.

5.___

6. The battle of Antietam is generally considered in hindsight to have been a
   A. total victory for the Union forces
   B. tactical victory for the Confederacy
   C. tactical draw, but a strategic defeat for the Confederacy
   D. tactical draw, but a strategic defeat for the Union

6.___

7. In 1864, the greatest threat to the military strength of   7.___
the Union was the
   A. rising tide of Copperhead sentiment throughout the
      Midwest
   B. high rate of desertion
   C. enormous casualty rate of Grant's Virginia campaigns
   D. end of the three-year enlistments that composed
      roughly half of Union forces

8. Confederates justified secession in 1860-1861 based upon   8.___
the
   A. writ of *habeas corpus*
   B. preamble of the Constitution
   C. slave tariff
   D. supreme-law clause of the Constitution

9. Which of the following states refused to ratify the 13th   9.___
Amendment to the Constitution in 1864?
   A. Missouri   B. Tennessee   C. Kentucky   D. Louisiana

10. Two days after his signing of the preliminary Emancipa-   10.___
tion Proclamation, which of the following edicts was
added by President Lincoln?
The
   A. suspension of the writ of habeas corpus in certain
      regions
   B. justification of emancipation on military grounds
   C. suspension of the Atlantic slave trade
   D. endorsement of voluntary colonization of freed slaves

11. As the Southern states began to secede from the Union in   11.___
1861, the initial strategic response on the part of most
Republicans was to
   A. capitulate on the question of the slave trade
   B. reinforce all government and military installations
      that had not yet been seized
   C. sit tight and do nothing to encourage secessionists
      or to alienate Southern Unionists
   D. retake government and military installations that
      had been seized

12. The strongest defensive works of the war were constructed   12.___
at
   A. Vicksburg   B. Chancellorsville
   C. Gettysburg   D. Appomattox

13. Upon taking command of the Union's Army of the Potomac   13.___
in 1861, Gen. George McClellan initially succeeded in
   A. replacing most regimental and company officers
   B. instilling lost pride and discipline
   C. winning new recruits to the Union cause
   D. launching a successful offensive into Confederate
      territory

14. While terrorist groups such as the Ku Klux Klan grew 　　　　14.___
    stronger and bolder in the South during 1868, federal
    troops were generally ineffective in dealing with the
    new wave of violence, primarily because
    　　A. membership in these groups was too large for them to
    　　　　be stopped
    　　B. martial law was now impossible in newly *reconstructed*
    　　　　states
    　　C. federal troops were generally held in check by
    　　　　President Johnson
    　　D. such groups enjoyed broad-based popular support

15. In the agricultural system that existed in the South 　　　15.___
    prior to the war, a *factor* or commission merchant served
    each of the following purposes EXCEPT
    　　A. advancing credit to the planter
    　　B. directly purchasing crops in times of surplus
    　　C. taking charge of the planter's crop when it reached
    　　　　an urban center
    　　D. serving as the planter's purchasing agent to obtain
    　　　　consumer goods

16. Approximately what percentage of Union soldiers who 　　　　16.___
    fought in the war were conscripts?
    　　A. 10　　　　　B. 25　　　　　C. 40　　　　　D. 55

17. President Lincoln's ＿＿＿ effectively constituted the 　　　17.___
    declaration of war that began the Civil War conflict.
    　　A. ordering of a naval blockade of the South
    　　B. expansion of regular army and naval forces beyond
    　　　　the number authorized by law
    　　C. issuance of the Emancipation Proclamation
    　　D. suspension of the writ of *habeas corpus* in parts of
    　　　　the country

18. Which of the following states adopted black suffrage by 　　18.___
    referendum in 1868?
    　　A. Arkansas　　B. Wisconsin　C. Iowa　　　　D. Missouri

19. Approximately what percentage of Civil War battle 　　　　19.___
    casualties were infantry soldiers?
    　　A. 25-35　　　B. 45-55　　　C. 60-70　　　D. 80-90

20. The PRIMARY reason for the overcrowding of Confederate 　　20.___
    prisons with Union soldiers in 1864 was the
    　　A. Confederate desire to inflict suffering on Union
    　　　　soldiers
    　　B. breakdown of the prisoner exchange program
    　　C. lack of Confederate resources for building and main-
    　　　　taining prison facilities
    　　D. lack of officers willing to oversee military prisons

21. The clearest explanation for why President Lincoln did   21.___
    not proclaim the war to be fought for the freedom of
    slaves, as well as for the preservation of the Union,
    was that he
    A. wanted to retain the favor of European governments
    B. still considered himself bound by the constitutional
       guarantee of slavery in the states
    C. was personally sympathetic to the cause of slavery
    D. wanted to retain the allegiance of Northern Democrats

22. Which Union general led the victory at Gettysburg?   22.___
    A. William S. Rosecrans   B. George Armstrong Custer
    C. Joseph Hooker   D. George Gordon Meade

23. During the period of modernization that occurred in the   23.___
    United States economy, the first and probably most impor-
    tant changes came in the sector of
    A. communications   B. agriculture
    C. steel production   D. transportation

24. Each of the following states abolished slavery before the   24.___
    end of the war EXCEPT
    A. Arkansas   B. Delaware   C. Louisiana D. Maryland

25. During the first two years of the war, European liberals   25.___
    became increasingly disillusioned with the Union cause,
    mostly because
    A. President Lincoln had frequently overstepped the
       authority of his office in the prosecution of the
       war and civil liberties had been widely violated
    B. Union soldiers were pillaging and confiscating
       Southern property on their campaigns
    C. the war was ostensibly being fought to restore a
       slaveholding Union
    D. the writ of *habeas corpus* had been suspended in
       certain regions

26. The first year that blacks were allowed in congressional   26.___
    galleries in the United States was
    A. 1860   B. 1862   C. 1864   D. 1866

27. The _____ was NOT mentioned in the platform developed at   27.___
    the 1864 Democratic Convention in Chicago.
    A. restoration of the writ of *habeas corpus*
    B. recognition of the states' rights to practice slavery
    C. immediate end of the war
    D. restoration of the Union as a condition for peace

28. Approximately how many Union soldiers lost their lives   28.___
    in the war?
    A. 120,000   B. 250,000   C. 360,000   D. 430,000

29. At the start of the Civil War, the manpower pool of the   29.___
    South was approximately _____ that of the North's.
    A. one-eighth   B. one-third
    C. three-quarters   D. the same as

30. The movement to impeach President Johnson, stoked by   30.___
    Republicans, was finally accomplished on the grounds that
    A. the President was guilty of conduct that was harmful
       to the public
    B. the President had violated the Tenure of Office Act
       by suspending a Cabinet member without congressional
       approval
    C. the President had criminally conspired with ex-
       Confederate officials to affect the fall of several
       Southern Republican regimes
    D. President Johnson had committed a grave misuse of his
       executive powers

31. Which of the following offers the best explanation for the   31.___
    Union defeat at the second Battle of Bull Run in the
    summer of 1862?
    A. A lack of coordination due to tensions between the
       Union commanders, Generals Pope and McClellan
    B. Inferior Union intelligence about the location and
       strength of Confederate troops
    C. The military brilliance of Robert E. Lee and Stonewall
       Jackson
    D. The better-trained and more disciplined Confederate
       infantry

32. During the 1830s, the *Second Great Awakening* in the anti-   32.___
    slavery movement was led in the North by religious
    A. Methodists   B. Calvinists
    C. Anabaptists   D. Quakers

33. Which of the following Confederate generals was from the   33.___
    western region of the United States?
    A. Robert E. Lee   B. Nathan Bedford Forrest
    C. Stonewall Jackson   D. James Longstreet

34. Albert Sidney Johnston, commander of the western Confe-   34.___
    derate forces, decided to attack General Grant's troops
    at Shiloh in 1862 in order to
    A. drive Union forces out of Tennessee with one swift
       surprise offensive
    B. regain the initiative before Grant's troops could be
       reinforced
    C. stall for time until his forces could be reinforced
       by General Beauregard
    D. stall for time while other Confederate troops
       destroyed bridges over the Tennessee River

35. Though sometimes used interchangeably, the terms *Copper-*   35.___
    heads and *Peace Democrats* can be differentiated in the
    following way:
    A. Copperheads tended to support Lincoln's suspension of
       the writ of *habeas corpus*
    B. Copperheads were generally more opposed to emancipa-
       tion
    C. Peace Democrats openly encouraged desertions from
       the Union army
    D. Peace Democrats were generally less supportive of the
       fugitive slave law

36. The Confederacy's war effort was financed primarily through 36.___
    each of the following EXCEPT
    A. taxation   B. treasury notes
    C. tariffs   D. loans

37. The opposition factions that surfaced within the Confe-   37.___
    derate government that hindered its effectiveness in the
    last half of the war was fueled by each of the following
    developments EXCEPT
    A. the suspension of the writ of *habeas corpus*
    B. the impressment of supplies
    C. the lack of movement against the corrupt profiteering
       trade
    D. conscription

38. A significant difference between the organization of   38.___
    Union and Confederate armies was that the Union
    A. government supplied the horses for its cavalry and
       artillery
    B. army had a greater complement of officers trained at
       military academies
    C. army used brigadier generals in its command structure
    D. army relied heavily on volunteer regiments

39. Which of the following military campaigns is generally   39.___
    considered to have been the MOST successful of the war?
    A. Lee's Shenandoah Valley campaign
    B. McClellan's peninsula campaign
    C. The Confederate invasion of Kentucky
    D. Grant's Vicksburg campaign

40. The *black codes* adopted by Southern governments after the 40.___
    war were generally harshest in South Carolina and
    A. Mississippi   B. North Carolina
    C. Kentucky   D. Georgia

41. In August of 1862, President Lincoln met with several   41.___
    black leaders in the White House and spoke with them of
    his ideas concerning the post-war situation among freed
    slaves. The position he advocated most strongly during
    this meeting was the
    A. migration of all freed slaves to Northern states
    B. separate colonization of freed slaves

    C. integration of freed slaves into white society, but
       with segregated institutions
    D. forced integration of freed slaves into white society
       and institutions

42. At the outset of the war, the Confederacy's most impor-   42.___
    tant advantage stemmed from its
    A. manpower   B. superior intelligence
    C. morale   D. defensive posture

43. Why did reconstruction's *carpetbag* Republican regimes   43.___
    begin to lose support in the North during the 1870s?
    A. Disillusionment with corrupt and mismanaged radical
       regimes
    B. Renewal of pro-slavery sentiment
    C. Disillusionment with the Grant administration
    D. Growing sympathy for the conquered South

44. The most frequently offered explanation for the failure   44.___
    of Union General George McClellan's peninsular campaign
    of 1862 is that
    A. he hesitated too long before launching his offensive
    B. he was strategically outsmarted by the Confederate
       commanders, Generals Lee and Jackson
    C. he was forced to withdraw troops for the defense of
       Washington
    D. his forces were outnumbered

45. Which of the following Confederate generals was replaced   45.___
    by Joseph Johnston after the battles of Chattanooga in
    1862?
    A. Pierre Gustav T. Beauregard
    B. John C. Breckinridge
    C. Simon Buckner
    D. Braxton Bragg

46. Which of the following events most clearly sparked the   46.___
    birth and rise of the Republican party?
    The
    A. Compromise of 1850   B. Kansas-Nebraska Act
    C. Fugitive Slave Law   D. Harper's Ferry massacre

47. In what year did the Confederacy unify command of its   47.___
    military forces under Robert E. Lee?
    A. 1861   B. 1862   C. 1864   D. 1865

48. The Union forces increased by a little over 500,000   48.___
    during the summer of 1862, due largely to the
    A. imposition of state quotas by the federal government
    B. recruitment of volunteers
    C. loyalty of Southern Unionists
    D. implementation of a national conscription act

49. In what year did the North adopt the Enrollment Act as its federal conscription law?
    A. 1861   B. 1862   C. 1863   D. 1864

50. Which of the following events in 1861 served as an official Union reaffirmation that it had no purpose, directly or indirectly, to interfere with slavery in the states where it existed?
    A. President Lincoln's pledge of continued enforcement of the fugitive slave law
    B. The Wilmot Proviso
    C. The Walker Tariff
    D. The Crittenden-Johnson resolution

KEY (CORRECT ANSWERS)

1. B	11. C	21. B	31. A	41. B
2. B	12. A	22. D	32. B	42. D
3. B	13. B	23. D	33. B	43. A
4. A	14. B	24. B	34. B	44. A
5. B	15. B	25. C	35. B	45. D
6. C	16. A	26. C	36. C	46. B
7. D	17. A	27. D	37. C	47. D
8. D	18. C	28. C	38. A	48. A
9. C	19. D	29. B	39. D	49. C
10. A	20. B	30. B	40. A	50. D

TEST 2

DIRECTIONS: Each question or incomplete statement is followed by several suggested answers or completions. Select the one that BEST answers the question or completes the statement. *PRINT THE LETTER OF THE CORRECT ANSWER IN THE SPACE AT THE RIGHT.*

1. The event which most clearly brought about President   1.___
   Lincoln's decision to issue the Emancipation Proclamation
   was
   A. the Confederate invasion of Kentucky
   B. the Battle of Antietam
   C. pressure from Northern Democrats prior to the 1862
      elections
   D. the Crittenden-Johnson resolution

2. Which of the following Union generals led troops at the   2.___
   battle of Chancellorsville?
   A. Ulysses S. Grant   B. George McClellan
   C. Joseph Hooker   D. George Gordon Meade

3. The battle of the Monitor against the Virginia (Merrimack),   3.___
   the first naval battle between ironclad ships, was signi-
   ficant in terms of the Civil War because it marked
   A. a major swing in the momentum of the naval war
   B. the turning of Confederate sentiment away from war
   C. the beginning of an all-out naval assault against
      Union ports
   D. the end of any Confederate salt-water challenges
      to the Union navy

4. No matter what their motives, Confederate opponents of   4.___
   Jefferson Davis's leadership throughout the latter half
   of the war most often expressed their dissent in terms of
   A. morality   B. economics
   C. military necessity   D. states' rights

5. In 1860, a Confederate act was passed to continue in   5.___
   force all the laws of the United States, so far as they
   were not inconsistent with the Confederate constitution.
   Which of the following states voted AGAINST this legislation?
   A. Georgia   B. South Carolina
   C. Mississippi   D. Virginia

6. The purpose of the Dix-Hill cartel of 1862 was to   6.___
   A. effect the release of all prisoners of war and
      address the problem of a unilateral excess of
      prisoners
   B. reach an agreement on the military seizure of private
      property

C. reach an agreement on the treatment of black prisoners of war

D. discuss a bilateral solution to the problem of profiteering

7. During the first half of the 19th century, the most fundamental reason for the South's failure to keep pace with modernization in the rest of the country was

    7.___

    A. a low literacy rate
    B. the expense of perpetuating the slave trade
    C. protectionist tariffs
    D. the lack of diversity in its economy

8. Which of the following best describes the federal law established by the Fifteenth Amendment to the Constitution, passed by Congress in 1869?
The

    8.___

    A. prohibition of states to deny citizens the right to vote on grounds of race, color, or previous condition of servitude
    B. affirmation that all male citizens aged twenty-one years or older had the right to vote
    C. prohibition of racial discrimination in providing suffrage and the prohibition of literacy, property, or nativity qualifications for suffrage
    D. prohibition of states to deny citizens the right to vote on grounds of race, color, previous condition of servitude, creed, or gender

9. Approximately what percentage of the total Confederate population was comprised by slaves?

    9.___

    A. 10   B. 20   C. 40   D. 50

10. Black suffrage suffered a setback in 1865, when the issue was defeated in referendums held in several Northern states. Which of the following states did not hold a referendum on the issue in 1865?

    10.___

    A. Wisconsin   B. Ohio
    C. Connecticut   D. Minnesota

11. In the beginning years of the Civil War, officers in volunteer companies were selected by means of

    11.___

    A. appointment by a state governor
    B. appointment by a regimental officer
    C. election by soldiers of the company
    D. achievement on written qualification examinations

12. Immediately following the war, all Republicans - radical, moderate, and conservative - generally agreed that

    12.___

    A. Southern representatives should not be admitted to Congress
    B. Southern states should be restored to the Union as quickly as possible
    C. freedmen should participate as much as possible in the reconstruction of the states
    D. freedmen should be granted immediate suffrage

13. In which of the following states were slaves freed by   13.___
    state legislation, rather than by implementation of the
    Emancipation Proclamation?
        A. Tennessee B. Texas   C. Kentucky   D. Arkansas

14. Although many white Union soldiers initially resisted the   14.___
    policy of arming blacks for the war, most of them
    eventually embraced it because
        A. they found the abolitionist rhetoric of Republican
           radicals to be persuasive
        B. it increased the probability of commissions for white
           officers
        C. they could become increasingly rich as *bounty brokers*
        D. it was the only way to turn the tide of the war to
           the Union's favor

15. Prior to its establishment at Richmond, the Confederate   15.___
    capital was in the city of
        A. Charlotte   B. Montgomery
        C. Atlanta   D. Columbia

16. During the 1864 election campaign, Republican politicians   16.___
    and sympathizers were able to damage the prospects of the
    Democratic party by means of
        A. focusing on the war record of the Democratic candi-
           date, George McClellan
        B. implicating Democrats in treasonous Copperhead
           conspiracy
        C. publicizing the high rate of military desertion in
           Midwestern states
        D. publicizing the pro-slavery sentiments of many
           Democrats

17. When the Freedmen's Bureau was finally established in   17.___
    1865, it was placed under the authority of the _____
    Department.
        A. Interior   B. War   C. Justice   D. Treasury

18. Which of the following was the most decisive issue that   18.___
    led to James K. Polk's nomination as Democratic presiden-
    tial candidate for the 1844 election?
        A. The annexation of Texas
        B. The negotiation of an Oregon territory
        C. The status of the New Mexico territory
        D. California statehood

19. Prior to its transfer to the War Department after the   19.___
    Emancipation Proclamation in 1862, which Union cabinet
    department was responsible for internal security?
        A. Interior   B. Treasury   C. State   D. Justice

20. In 1864, after the North developed a unified command   20. ___
    system (under General Grant) to coordinate strategy
    on all fronts, which of the following was NOT a component
    of the original strategic plan devised by this command?
    General
    A. Benjamin Butler would move troops up the James River
       to threaten Richmond
    B. Meade was to lead the Army of the Potomac in attack-
       ing General Lee's Army of Virginia
    C. Sherman would lead a march through Georgia to cut
       off the Confederate troops from resources
    D. Sigel was to move up the Shenandoah Valley to prevent
       aid from reaching Lee's army

21. The first state to secede from the Union, in 1860, was   21. ___
    A. Virginia   B. South Carolina
    C. Tennessee   D. Georgia

22. The Thirteenth Amendment changed the substance of Consti-   22. ___
    tutional amendments by establishing a precedent for
    A. limiting the claims of the citizenry upon certain
       types of personal property
    B. limiting the power of the federal government
    C. defining the terms of permissible revolutionary or
       anti-government activities
    D. restricting state powers or expanding those of the
       national government

23. During the first years of the war, Union abolitionists   23. ___
    proposed the legitimate freeing of slaves, in spite of
    the constitutional guarantee, by means of
    A. a simple declaration of the illegitimacy of slavery
    B. confiscating slaves as enemy property that was being
       used in direct aid of the rebellion
    C. enlisting as many slaves as possible in the Union
       armies
    D. a constitutional amendment

24. Which of the following Confederate generals led the   24. ___
    unsuccessful campaign against Union forces at Nashville
    in 1864?
    A. William J. Hardee   B. Jeb Stuart
    C. John B. Hood   D. Joseph E. Johnston

25. The 1862 battle in which the combined casualty rate   25. ___
    (33% of Union troops lost; 31% of Confederate troops)
    was the highest of the war was fought at
    A. Gettysburg   B. Chancellorsville
    C. Vicksburg   D. Stone's River

26. The Wade-Davis Bill of 1864 was a source of extreme   26.___
    political friction between the President and the legis-
    lature. This friction centered on the issue of
       A. capricious use of the Presidential veto
       B. popular sovereignty
       C. punishment of revolutionaries
       D. the President's selective application of legislation
          that had been approved by Congress

27. Which of the following was NOT a characteristic of the   27.___
    antebellum United States?
       A. Expanded education and mass communications
       B. A marked decrease in agricultural products
       C. Rapid increases in industrial output per capita
       D. A value system that emphasized change over tradition

28. Which commodity, according to most estimates, was respon-   28.___
    sible for the greatest amount of revenue during the
    corrupt profiteering practices of the war?
       A. Cotton   B. Steel   C. Whiskey   D. Wheat

29. The 1861-1862 Union campaign into Kentucky, which   29.___
    resulted in the capture of Forts Henry and Donelson,
    was commanded by Generals
       A. Halleck and Buell   B. Buell and Grant
       C. Sherman and Grant   D. McClellan and Sherman

30. The passage of the Enrollment Act, the Union's federal   30.___
    conscription law, sparked major antidraft and antiblack
    rioting in the city of
       A. Cincinnati   B. New York
       C. Philadelphia   D. Washington

31. As the Fort Sumter crisis intensified in 1861, Secretary   31.___
    of State William Seward recommended to President Lincoln
    that the situation might be defused by
       A. leaving soldiers stationed at Fort Moultrie where
          they were, without increasing the staffing at Fort
          Sumter
       B. allowing states the right to self-determination on
          the issue of slavery
       C. engaging in a foreign war over violations of the
          Monroe Doctrine
       D. abandoning Fort Sumter to the Confederacy

32. In what city did the Republicans hold their 1864 conven-   32.___
    tion?
       A. Baltimore   B. Cincinnati
       C. Chicago   D. New York

33. Which of the following was a result of the Compromise of   33.___
    1877?
       A. The rapid mobilization of Southern state militias
       B. A run-off vote in the presidential election

C. Suffrage for all adult black males
D. The collapse of all remaining reconstruction governments in the South

34. The bloodiest single day of the war, in which nearly   34.___
    5,000 soldiers died on both sides, occurred during the
    battle of
       A. Vicksburg   B. Gettysburg
       C. Shiloh   D. Antietam

35. President Johnson's 1865 proclamations concerning   35.___
    reconstruction proposed each of the following EXCEPT
       A. restitution of all property except slaves to those
          taking an oath of allegiance to the Union
       B. naming a provisional governor in North Carolina
       C. recognition of Lincoln-sponsored governments in
          Louisiana, Arkansas, and Tennessee
       D. provision of a universal plan for the education of
          freedmen

36. Approximately what portion of the entire Confederate   36.___
    fighting force was made up of soldiers enlisted through
    conscription?
    One-
       A. eighth   B. fifth   C. third   D. half

37. In the South, which of the following was a gradual effect 37.___
    of the end of the African slave trade (1808)?
       A. The expansion of slave labor into more skilled trades
       B. A reduction in the rate of slave population increase
       C. A greater effort to keep slave families together
       D. An improvement in the physical treatment of slaves

38. In composing the Reconstruction Act of 1867, radical and 38.___
    moderate Republicans generally agreed upon the issue of
       A. confiscation and redistribution of land to freedmen
       B. nullification of existing Southern governments
       C. long-term disenfranchisement of ex-Confederates
       D. federally-supported schools for Southern blacks

39. The region of the Union considered to be the *mother of* 39.___
    Republican radicalism throughout the war and reconstruc-
    tion years was
       A. the Great Lakes region
       B. New England
       C. the rural Pennsylvania-Ohio River and canal regions
       D. the border states

40. The Confederate decision in 1865 to arm slaves for battle 40.___
    resulted in
       A. the recruitment of black troops, but none actually
          serving in battle
       B. the formation and mobilization of a few small black
          regiments, but with no serious casualties

C. an internal attempt to overthrow the Confederate government

D. the death of several dozen black Confederate soldiers

41. As black troops were increasingly introduced into the Union army, President Lincoln originally planned to use them only for rear area duties, garrisoning forts, and protecting supply dumps. Which of the following was NOT a reason for this?

   41.___

A. Remaining skepticism about the suitability of black soldiers for combat

B. The belief that black soldiers were less likely to become sick during garrison duty than white soldiers

C. The lack of Northern resources to equip the additional forces for combat

D. Rear-area duties would reduce the possibility of capture

42. The first Congressional Republican attack on slavery in 1862 was

   42.___

A. the creation of schools for black children in Washington

B. an article of war prohibiting army officers from returning fugitive slaves to their masters

C. the prohibition of slavery in all territories

D. the abolition of slavery in the District of Columbia

43. From the period of 1860-1870, it is estimated that the material wealth of the South decreased by about _____ percent.

   43.___

A. 15   B. 25   C. 40   D. 60

44. Which of the following was not an element of the Compromise of 1850?
The

   44.___

A. admission of California as a state

B. banning of slavery in the New Mexico and Utah territories

C. abolition of the slave trade in the District of Columbia

D. adjustment of Texas's borders

45. Confederate soldiers and Georgia militiamen burned and destroyed large parts of the land and resources in 1864 in order to

   45.___

A. starve Sherman's troops on their way to Savannah

B. keep Confederate property from falling into Union hands

C. exact revenge from Southern slaves and sharecroppers in Georgia

D. drive slaves out of the path of Sherman's march

46. Throughout the war, the European country which demon-
strated the strongest pro-Southern sentiment was
    A. Spain   B. Britain   C. Portugal   D. France

    46.___

47. The last state to ratify the Fifteenth Amendment was
    A. Texas   B. Georgia
    C. Tennessee   D. South Carolina

    47.___

48. Throughout the war, armies on both sides preferred to
organize entirely new regiments instead of channeling
new recruits into old regiments to keep up to strength.
Which of the following were reasons for this?
    I. High casualties tended to eventually replace entire
       regiments anyway.
   II. New regiments provided state governors with a means
       of patronage.
  III. The primary basis for forming regiments would have
       been weakened by intermingling troops from different
       areas and groups.
   IV. New regiments provided ambitious men a means of
       advancement.

    The CORRECT answer is:
    A. I, III   B. II, IV
    C. II, III, IV   D. I, III, IV

    48.___

49. By the war's end, approximately _____ of the 3.5 million
Confederate slaves had been freed directly by Northern
invasion.
    A. 15,000   B. 450,000
    C. 1.5 million   D. 2.5 million

    49.___

50. At the height of reconstruction in the 1870's, approximately what percentage of all Southern officeholders
were black?
    A. 1-3   B. 15-20   C. 35-50   D. 60-70

    50.___

KEY (CORRECT ANSWERS)

1. B	11. C	21. B	31. C	41. C
2. C	12. A	22. D	32. A	42. B
3. D	13. A	23. B	33. D	43. D
4. D	14. B	24. C	34. D	44. B
5. B	15. B	25. D	35. D	45. A
6. A	16. B	26. D	36. C	46. D
7. D	17. B	27. B	37. D	47. B
8. A	18. A	28. C	38. B	48. C
9. C	19. C	29. B	39. B	49. C
10. B	20. C	30. B	40. A	50. B

TEST 3

1. Which religious group played the most significant role in the 18th-century beginnings of the antislavery movement in America?
   A. Shakers   B. Mormons   C. Quakers   D. Catholics

   1.___

2. General William T. Sherman's famous march came to an end in 1865 in the city of
   A. Columbia   B. Wilmington
   C. Savannah   D. Raleigh

   2.___

3. The North's assurances of a quick victory in 1862 were initially cut short by
   A. Stonewall Jackson's Shenandoah Valley campaign
   B. General McClellan's failure to capture Richmond
   C. the second battle of Manassas
   D. the battle of Shiloh

   3.___

4. The military successes of the 1864 Union campaign into Virginia were slowed when
   A. General Lee led a brilliant counteroffensive that temporarily divided the Union armies
   B. General Lee ordered his troops into defensive positions in trenches
   C. General Sheridan's cavalry moved in from the rear to join the fight
   D. a shocking number of Union troops were killed at Cold Harbor

   4.___

5. Which of the following departments was NOT included in the Confederate cabinet?
   A. War   B. Interior   C. State   D. Justice

   5.___

6. During the Union's military campaign of 1864, General Philip Sheridan's responsibility was to
   A. reduce and devastate the Shenandoah Valley
   B. command the Army of the Potomac
   C. engage Confederate troops east of Richmond
   D. delay Johnston's troops in northwestern Georgia

   6.___

7. The Union navy's chief task throughout the Civil War was
   A. to use inland waterways to transport troops deep into the Confederacy
   B. the blockade of Southern ports
   C. the defense of Northern ports
   D. to seize Southern ports

   7.___

8. The *scalawags* of Southern reconstruction were drawn
   largely from each of the following regions EXCEPT
      A. western North Carolina and Virginia
      B. upland counties of eastern Tennessee
      C. eastern Texas
      D. northern Georgia, Alabama, and Arkansas

8.____

9. In 1862, the battle of Fredericksburg brought to head a
   political crisis within the Lincoln administration that
   centered on the
      A. conduct of Secretary of the Treasury Salmon P. Chase
         in securing financing for the war effort
      B. power of the executive over legislative due process
      C. influence of Secretary of State Seward on questions
         concerning slavery and military appointments
      D. polity of imposing the Emancipation Proclamation on
         an already rebellious Confederacy

9.____

10. Which of the following Southern cities offered great
    strategic importance by forming the junction of the
    Confederacy's two east-west railroads, as well as the
    gateway to the war industries of Georgia?
       A. Chattanooga   B. Nashville
       C. Murfreesboro   D. Vicksburg

10.____

11. Which of the following was NOT thought to be either an
    immediate or eventual consequence of the first battle
    of Manassas (Bull Run) in 1861?
       A. Northern optimism concerning its artillery troops
       B. A sense of inferiority among Northern officers
       C. Southern overconfidence on the home front
       D. Strengthened Northern determination

11.____

12. The Union general who led the drive through central
    Tennessee in 1862 was
       A. William T. Sherman   B. William S. Rosecrans
       C. Ambrose Burnside   D. Joseph Hooker

12.____

13. Each of the following was a factor in the weakening of
    the Whig party in the South during the 1840s and 1850s
    EXCEPT the
       A. defections to nativist parties in 1854-1855
       B. failure to pass an effective fugitive slave law
       C. increasing perception of Democrats as stronger
          Southern rights advocates
       D. memory of Whig President Zachary Taylor's admission
          of California and New Mexico as states

13.____

14. In general, the ratio of Civil War soldiers who died of
    disease to those killed in battle was about
       A. 1:2   B. 1:1   C. 2:1   D. 5:1

14.____

15. It is generally true that the policies of European govern- 15.___
ments toward the Civil War were determined ultimately by
    A. considerations of power and self-interest
    B. questions of ideology concerning government and
       sovereignty
    C. public opinion
    D. stances on the issue of slavery

16. The absence of political parties in the Confederate 16.___
government system ultimately served to
    A. create a more unified front against the Union cause
    B. alienate most of the Southern aristocracy
    C. encourage corruption through its lack of consequence
    D. produce an opposition that was unmanageable

17. Which of the following Confederate cities was captured by 17.___
Union Admiral David Farragut in 1862?
    A. Vicksburg   B. Charleston
    C. New Orleans   D. Mobile

18. The Republican party was founded in 1854 having its main 18.___
issue the prohibition of
    A. slavery throughout the United States
    B. slavery in newly acquired territories
    C. slavery in the District of Columbia
    D. the slave trade throughout the United States

19. Which of the following military leaders was NOT involved 19.___
in the 1862 battle at Stone's River?
    A. William T. Sherman   B. George Thomas
    C. John C. Breckinridge   D. Braxton Bragg

20. The Democratic Convention of 1864 affected the Republican 20.___
Party by
    A. weakening Republican standing by creating a united
       Democratic front
    B. weakening Republican opposition by creating a Copper-
       head splinter in the Democratic Party
    C. helping splinter the Republican Party into feuding
       factions
    D. helping to consolidate Republican factions against
       political opposition

21. In 1865, which of the following states was represented 21.___
in both the Confederate and Union cabinets?
    A. Kentucky   B. West Virginia
    C. Tennessee   D. Missouri

22. When William T. Sherman negotiated surrender with Joseph 22.___
Johnston in 1865, each of the following was a condition
proposed by Sherman EXCEPT the
    A. recognition of Southern state governments when their
       officials had taken an oath of allegiance
    B. guarantee of Southerners to political rights and
       franchises

C. allowance of disbanded Confederate troops to deposit
   their arms in state arsenals
D. immediate freedom of all slaves

23. The most significant way in which slavery inhibited the
    advance of modernization in the South was
    A. its extreme limitation of the upward mobility of
       slaves in the labor force
    B. the expense of purchasing and maintaining slaves
    C. its degradation of the status of labor among the
       general working population
    D. its perpetuation of the Southern reliance on
       agriculture

23.___

24. In 1864, Confederate general Jeb Stuart was killed by
    General
    A. Sheridan's cavalry raid at Yellow Tavern
    B. Meade's troops at Spotsylvania
    C. Sigel's troops in the Shenandoah
    D. Butler's troops on the James River

24.___

25. In the spring of 1862, Confederate General Thomas J.
    "Stonewall" Jackson died of pneumonia, which had set
    in after he was wounded at the battle of
    A. Fredericksburg   B. Chattanooga
    C. Chancellorsville   D. Gettysburg

25.___

26. The last major Confederate port to be sealed off by
    Union troops was
    A. Charleston   B. Wilmington
    C. Port Royal   D. Mobile

26.___

27. Which state was won by Stephen Douglas during the 1860
    presidential election?
    A. Missouri   B. South Carolina
    C. Florida   D. Ohio

27.___

28. Which of the following most strongly supported Democratic
    candidate George McClellan in the presidential election
    of 1864?
      I. Protestant denominational groups
     II. Rural areas in which the foreign element dominated
    III. The immigrant proletariat
     IV. Skilled urban workers and professional classes

    The CORRECT answer is:
      A. I, II   B. II, III   C. I, IV   D. IV *only*

28.___

29. It is generally believed today that President Johnson's
    liberal granting of pardons to Southerners immediately
    following the war was most evidently a result of his
    A. desire to create an atmosphere of goodwill and
       reconciliation
    B. latent pro-slavery sentiments

29.___

C. susceptibility to flattery and a growing bitterness toward Republicans

D. hope for providing a Southern political counter-weight to corrupt carpetbag regimes

30. Upon his election to the presidency, each of the following qualities displayed by President Lincoln tended to create an unfavorable impression EXCEPT his
    A. preoccupation with office-seekers at the expense of weightier matters
    B. social awkwardness
    C. inability to take a strong political stand on the question of union
    D. caution in making decisions

30.___

31. At the outset of the war, the Confederacy's biggest military weakness was in the area of
    A. the overall training and readiness of officers
    B. naval power
    C. morale
    D. cavalry

31.___

32. General McClellan was ultimately removed from command of the Army of the Potomac because of his
    A. Democratic politics
    B. inability to inspire his troops
    C. inability to carry out successful military operations
    D. vocal pro-slavery stance

32.___

33. Throughout the war, the rate of death from disease of black Union troops was approximately _____ that of Northern white soldiers.
    A. one-half   B. the same
    C. twice   D. four times

33.___

34. The main reason behind Britain's negotiation of a treaty of recognition and commerce with the Republic of Texas in the 1840s was to
    A. foster a British-Texan slave trade
    B. promote emancipation through British influence
    C. provoke a civil conflict that would weaken the United States
    D. prevent its annexation as a slave state

34.___

35. Despite President Johnson's impeachment in 1868, the President was ultimately acquitted for the reason that
    A. he used powers that were clearly discretionary
    B. he was found not to have violated the spirit of the Tenure of Office Act
    C. he managed to build a strong following among Democrats and conservative Republicans
    D. moderate congressmen did not want to weaken the institution of the executive

35.___

36. The first Confederate state capital to fall to the North   36.____
    was
    A. Little Rock   B. Frankfort
    C. Columbia   D. Nashville

37. President Lincoln's solution to the Fort Sumter crisis   37.____
    was to
    A. arm the fort heavily in anticipation of a Union
       offensive into Confederate territory
    B. send the troops at the fort only food and supplies
       through unarmed transports, in order to test
       Confederate aggression
    C. abandon the fort in the hope of preserving the Union
    D. do nothing and wait for the Confederacy to attack

38. Which of the following Confederate generals nearly   38.____
    captured Washington in 1864?
    A. Jeb Stuart   B. Jubal Early
    C. James Longstreet   D. Robert E. Lee

39. The behavior of the Confederate Vice President, Alexander   39.____
    H. Stephens, throughout the war can best be described as
    demonstrating
    A. a constant overemphasis on military matters
    B. continued attempts to undermine the Confederate
       executive
    C. thinly veiled sympathy for the cause of union
    D. unqualified support for the administration

40. The first Confederate invasion of the North occurred   40.____
    with the battle of
    A. Gettysburg   B. Perryville
    C. Antietam   D. Corinth

41. Which of the following was NOT an element of the original   41.____
    conscription law, the Enrollment Act, passed by the Union?
    A. The allowance of substitution
    B. Various occupational exemptions
    C. The permission of a drafted man to pay a commutation
       fee rather than serve
    D. The stimulation of volunteering through the offering
       of bounties

42. Which 1846 proposal advocated the banning of slavery from   42.____
    any territories that might be annexed as a result of the
    Mexican War?
    The
    A. Missouri Compromise   B. Kansas-Nebraska Act
    C. Wilmot Proviso   D. Walker Tariff

43. As the issue of black suffrage was discussed during the   43.____
    early years of reconstruction, President Johnson voiced
    an unwillingness to include former black Union soldiers
    in the electorate. What was his reason for this?

A. Their inclusion would have doubled the size of the black electorate.
B. Black soldiers were the most humiliating symbol of Southern defeat.
C. Their inclusion would threaten the security of reconstruction governments.
D. Black soldiers were generally better educated than other blacks.

44. The event or situation that most clearly turned Southern-   44.___
ers against the cause of the Confederacy was
    A. mistreatment of Union prisoners of war
    B. the operation of the conscription act
    C. the burden of Confederate wartime taxation
    D. slavery

45. Approximately what percentage of Union soldiers deserted   45.___
during the war?
    A. 2   B. 10   C. 15   D. 20

46. The main port of entry for runners of the Union blockade   46.___
was the city of
    A. Port Royal   B. Norfolk
    C. Wilmington   D. Charleston

47. Which of the following best describes an effect of the   47.___
battle at Cold Harbor in 1864?
    A. Intensification of the peace movement and the oppo-
       sition to Lincoln in the North
    B. The alteration of General Lee's strategy to en-
       trenched defense rather than mobilized offensives
    C. Heightened criticism of Jefferson Davis from high-
       level Confederate officials
    D. The decimation of the Union cavalry

48. The National Union movement, formed in 1866 to form a   48.___
conservative (pro-Johnson) coalition in the United States
government, ultimately failed because of several essential weaknesses. Which of the following was not one of
these weaknesses?
    A. The increasing stridency of Andrew Johnson himself
    B. Domination of the movement by Democrats
    C. The universal popularity of radical Republicans
    D. The movement's exaggerated claim that Southerners
       were more obedient to the Constitution than
       Northerners

49. In the spring of 1862, General McClellan altered the   49.___
Union strategy by planning an elaborate flanking maneuver
with the Army of the Potomac against the Confederates at
Centreville. His plan resulted in one of the first major
disagreements to arise between McClellan and President
Lincoln.
The issue at the center of this disagreement was

A. the overall numerical strength of Confederate forces
B. the needless loss of life among Union soldiers
C. the alleged superiority of the Confederate cavalry
D. whether the objective of the Union forces should be
   to overwhelm the Confederate forces or to capture
   Richmond

50. Jefferson Davis's first secretary of state was   50.___
    A. R.M.T. Hunter   B. John C. Breckinridge
    C. Robert Toombs   D. Leroy P. Walker

——

KEY (CORRECT ANSWERS)

1. C	11. A	21. A	31. B	41. B
2. B	12. B	22. D	32. C	42. C
3. B	13. B	23. C	33. C	43. B
4. B	14. C	24. A	34. B	44. B
5. B	15. A	25. C	35. D	45. B
6. A	16. D	26. B	36. D	46. C
7. B	17. C	27. A	37. B	47. A
8. C	18. B	28. B	38. B	48. C
9. C	19. A	29. C	39. B	49. D
10. A	20. D	30. C	40. C	50. C

TEST 4

1. In 1864, General Ulysses S. Grant ordered that no more exchanges of Confederate prisoners of war would occur until certain conditions were met. Which of the following was/were the conditions of Grant's suspension? The
   I. end of Southern blockade-running
   II. end of Confederate discrimination against black prisoners
   III. end to the illicit profiteering trade
   IV. release of enough Union prisoners to offset the Confederates paroled after Vicksburg

   The CORRECT answer is:
   A. I *only*   B. I, III   C. II, IV   D. III, IV

   1.___

2. Which of the following battles in the western theater was considered to have been a tactical victory for the Confederates?
   A. Vicksburg   B. Corinth
   C. Chickamauga   D. Chattanooga

   2.___

3. From 1862-1864, Indiana Governor Oliver P. Morton ran the state without a legislature for the reason that
   A. all appropriations were being directed to the war effort
   B. Republicans had deserted the state senate in order to deny a Copperhead-dominated legislature
   C. Peace Democrats and Copperheads had boycotted all senate sessions in order to withdraw support from the war effort
   D. the 1862 elections had been suspended by the war

   3.___

4. Just prior to the war, approximately what percentage of United States industrial capacity was possessed by the North?
   A. 35   B. 60   C. 75   D. 90

   4.___

5. Of the following Southern states, which was the first to pass through reconstruction into *home rule*, or restored state sovereignty?
   A. North Carolina   B. Tennessee
   C. Georgia   D. Arkansas

   5.___

6. The most significant effect of the development of the 6.___
   canal system during the mid-19th century in America was
   A. the decreasing importance of rail transport
   B. the reduction in Northern reliance on Southern
      agriculture
   C. an overall reduction in imports
   D. the reorientation of trade patterns along east-west
      lines in the North

7. During the 1865 Hampton Roads peace conference between 7.___
   Abraham Lincoln and Alexander Stephens, each of the
   following was a term of surrender proposed by President
   Lincoln EXCEPT
   A. immediate reunion
   B. no compensation to Southerners for freed slaves
   C. no receding on the issue of emancipation
   D. an absolute end to hostilities and the disbanding
      of all forces

8. Which of the following was NOT among the principal killer 8.___
   diseases of the Civil War?
   A. Typhoid   B. Malaria   C. Dysentery   D. Influenza

9. Each of the following describes a policy held by President 9.___
   Lincoln at the outset of the Civil War EXCEPT
   A. opposition to the arming of blacks
   B. limited war
   C. gradual, compensated emancipation
   D. reconstruction of the Union

10. The 1864 event that most clearly strengthened support 10.___
    for President Lincoln's policies in the North was
    A. Sherman's march
    B. the Confederate loss of Jeb Stuart
    C. the fall of Atlanta
    D. the battle at Cold Harbor

11. The principal agency through which Northern women aided 11.___
    the war effort was the
    A. Young Women's Christian Association
    B. United States Sanitary Commission
    C. American Red Cross
    D. American Public Health Association

12. Each of the following was an element of President 12.___
    Lincoln's 1863 plan for reconstruction EXCEPT
    A. a full pardon to individuals involved in the war
    B. acceptance of the degree of emancipation already
       accomplished
    C. the confiscation of all private property used in
       direct or indirect aid of the war effort
    D. the political restoration of a state dependent upon
       an oath of allegiance from at least 10 percent of
       the voting population

13. Of the following political parties in the antebellum   13.___
    United States, which was NOT an abolitionist party?
       A. Free Soil   B. Republican
       C. Know-Nothing   D. Liberty

14. President Andrew Johnson's idea of reconstruction for   14.___
    the South included
       A. universal black suffrage
       B. the temporary designation of rebellious states to
          the status of territories
       C. reconstruction as primarily a legislative function
       D. the states' retention of all constitutional rights

15. It is generally believed that the Union attacks at the   15.___
    battle of Antietam failed because
       A. they were delivered serially instead of simultaneous-
          ly
       B. superior Confederate intelligence was able to locate
          and isolate the component forces
       C. the Union forces were outnumbered
       D. the Confederate forces could hold fast to a defen-
          sive position

16. During the Union's 1864 military campaigns in Virginia,   16.___
    the ratio of Union casualties to Confederate casualties
    was approximately
       A. 1:3   B. 1:2   C. 1:1   D. 2:1

17. In 1863, a dramatic upsurge in pro-Union opinion occurred   17.___
    in Britain, largely as a result of
       A. the battle of Antietam
       B. the Emancipation Proclamation
       C. the Confederate invasion of Kentucky
       D. Lincoln's suspension of the writ of *habeas corpus*

18. An immediate consequence of the war following the final   18.___
    surrender of the Confederacy was the
       A. trial and execution of several Confederates for
          treason
       B. continued buildup of state militias in both Northern
          and Southern states
       C. rapid demobilization of the Union armies
       D. election of a series of *military* United States Presi-
          dents

19. Which of the following were problems associated with the   19.___
    Confederate conscription law that was first passed in 1862?
        I. Overall resistance to what was perceived as an
           encroachment on states' rights
       II. Numerous exemption categories which favored the rich
      III. The tacit encouragement of violent impressment
       IV. A provision allowing one to escape military service
           by hiring a substitute

The CORRECT answer is:
A. I, III
B. II, IV
C. I, II, IV
D. II, III, IV

20. Approximately what percentage of Southern capital was invested in manufacturing at the outset of the war?

20.___

A. 3   B. 15   C. 50   D. 75

21. In general, it can be said that President Lincoln's idea of reconstruction for the South was based on the idea that the main task of reconstruction was to

21.___

A. restore control of the states to loyal citizens
B. maintain Northern political control over the new Southern governments
C. completely destroy the South's capacity for war
D. free all remaining slaves from servitude

22. Throughout the war, the Confederacy failed to achieve even diplomatic recognition by a single foreign government. The most important single factor in this failure was

22.___

A. the skill with which Union diplomats persuaded European governments away from the Confederate cause
B. generalized European opposition to the institution of slavery
C. fear of the consequences of war with the North
D. the inability of the Confederacy to win enough consecutive victories to convince observers of the possibility of sustained independence

23. Throughout the war, the period of the worst morale in the North is generally considered to have been the

23.___

A. summer of 1861   B. fall of 1862
C. winter of 1863   D. summer of 1864

24. Each of the following was an element of the Confederate constitution EXCEPT

24.___

A. the subordination of individual states to one central Confederate government
B. the guarantee of slavery in all territories and states
C. executive line-item veto power in appropriations bills
D. the prohibition of protective tariffs

25. Of all the Confederate territory covered by William T. Sherman's troops during 1864, the greatest amount of damage was inflicted upon

25.___

A. Georgia   B. South Carolina
C. North Carolina   D. Virginia

26. Which of the following Union generals took over command of the Army of the Potomac from George McClellan in 1862?

26.___

A. William T. Sherman   B. Ambrose E. Burnside
C. Henry Halleck   D. Ulysses S. Grant

27. The purpose of the 1854 Kansas-Nebraska Act was to   27.___
    A. ban slavery in the territories of Kansas and Nebraska
    B. refer the issue of slavery in Kansas and Nebraska to
       popular sovereignty
    C. enact fugitive slave laws in both Kansas and Nebraska
    D. repeal the Missouri Compromise's ban on slavery in the
       northern Louisiana Purchase territories

28. In the entire Union military campaign from the Wilderness   28.___
    to Cold Harbor in 1864, approximately how many Union
    soldiers were lost?
    A. 12,000   B. 30,000   C. 55,000   D. 72,000

29. The Confederate Impressment Act of 1863 ultimately   29.___
    resulted in the
    A. reduced role of speculators in commodity markets
    B. intensification of shortages and inflation through
       increased resistance on the part of farmers and
       merchants
    C. increasing desertion of Confederate soldiers
    D. alleviation of shortages and inflation through the
       arbitration of a fair price for goods

30. Which of the following states did NOT call a convention   30.___
    to discuss the issue of secession?
    A. Kentucky   B. Arkansas   C. Virginia   D. Missouri

31. In 1865, President Johnson and the Republicans argued   31.___
    over the issue of black suffrage. President Johnson
    claimed that interfering in a state's voting qualifica-
    tions was unconstitutional. Republicans responded that
    A. until a constitutional amendment could be adopted,
       they were in agreement
    B. the Constitution implied federal regulation of
       voting qualifications and standards
    C. it was no more unconstitutional than appointing
       provisional governors or abolishing slavery, which
       the executive had already done
    D. black suffrage was a moral issue, not a constitu-
       tional one

32. The reason for President Lincoln's extreme distress   32.___
    after the battle of Gettysburg was that
    A. Union forces continued to pursue Confederate forces
       across the Potomac
    B. the weakened Confederate army was not captured and
       destroyed after the battle
    C. Union generals continued to publicly criticize the
       President's leadership
    D. an appalling loss of life was suffered on both sides

33. The most decisive battle of Grant's 1862 Vicksburg   33.___
    campaign was fought at
    A. Jackson   B. Champion's Hill
    C. Big Black River   D. Vicksburg

34. In the spring of 1862, the Midwestern Copperhead politi-   34.___
cian Clement L. Vallandigham spoke out strongly in support
of a platform that included each of the following EXCEPT
the
A. unconstitutionality of conscription
B. repudiation of the Emancipation Proclamation
C. deportation of free blacks to the South
D. declaration of an armistice with the South and the
restoration of the Union

35. Militarily, the Confederacy enjoyed its greatest early   35.___
superiority in its
A. infantry   B. artillery
C. cavalry   D. volunteer pool

36. During the conferences of the Confederate cabinet and   36.___
generals in the spring of 1862, Robert E. Lee pushed
for the concentration of Confederate forces in the
Virginia theater. Each of the following was a reason
given for this plan EXCEPT
A. enabling the army to resupply itself from the
Pennsylvania countryside
B. possibly accomplishing the capture of Washington
C. relieving the threat to Richmond
D. accepting that the war in the West was probably lost

37. Which of the following countries was the first to abolish   37.___
slavery?
A. France   B. Britain
C. United States   D. Denmark

38. The most common reason given for the Union loss at the   38.___
battle of Chancellorsville in 1862 was that
A. Confederate General Lee did not divide his army
during the engagement
B. the Confederates outnumbered the Union forces
C. the Union troops attempted to travel over waterways
D. the full force of the Union Army was never engaged
at one time

39. The most frequent source of friction between the Confed-   39.___
erate government and Southern state officials regarding
the issue of states' rights was probably
A. taxation   B. the slave trade
C. the fugitive slave law D. conscription

40. Confederate General Joseph E. Johnston was relieved of   40.___
command in 1864 by Jefferson Davis, ostensibly for each
of the following reasons EXCEPT
A. he failed to come to the aid of Vicksburg's besieged
defenders in 1861
B. his troops retreated to Richmond before being rescued
by General Lee in 1862

C. he failed to fight his way out of Bull Run in the first battle of Manassas in 1861
D. he retreated from Sherman's armies all the way to Atlanta in 1864

41. Among volunteer regiments in both Union and Confederate armies, the principal basis for recruitment was most often
    A. geography B. class   C. ethnicity D. training

41.___

42. The election crisis of 1866 was caused by conflicting reports of results in each of the following states EXCEPT
    A. Florida   B. Georgia
    C. South Carolina   D. Louisiana

42.___

43. Each of the following is now considered to have been a condition that contributed to the deplorable disease-ridden condition of the Confederate prison camp at Andersonville, Georgia EXCEPT
    A. the extreme cruelty of Confederate guards
    B. the inability of Confederate officers to deal with the immense number of prisoners
    C. the poverty of the Confederacy in material resources
    D. Confederate difficulties in obtaining supplies and equipment

43.___

44. Which of the following states was NOT won by George McClellan in the presidential campaign of 1864?
    A. Kentucky   B. Delaware
    C. Ohio   D. New Jersey

44.___

45. Which of the following events most decisively led to the Compromise of 1850?
    The
    A. implementation of Oregon's territorial status
    B. annexation of Texas
    C. implementation of New Mexico's territorial status
    D. admission of California as a state

45.___

46. According to General William T. Sherman, the purpose of his armies' march to Savannah was primarily to
    A. destroy the civilian population's willingness to support the Confederate war effort
    B. capture a key Confederate port
    C. destroy the agricultural resources of the South
    D. capture a staging ground for his movement into South Carolina

46.___

47. By the end of the war, approximately what percentage of Union troops were black?
    A. 15   B. 25   C. 40   D. 60

47.___

48. Each of the following is generally considered to have   48.____
    been a reason for the generalized ineffectiveness of
    the Confederate Congress throughout the war EXCEPT
        A. a long tradition of obstructionism in legislature
        B. a tendency toward long sessions of rhetoric and
           oration
        C. the tendency of most powerful Confederate leaders
           to join the military
        D. flaws in the checks and balances provisions of the
           Confederate constitution

49. Of all the litigation that has occurred in the United   49.____
    States as a result of the Fourteenth Amendment, most of
    it has concerned Section
        A. 1, which defined all native-born persons as citizens
           and provided for equal protection of all citizens
           under the law
        B. 2, which provided for the proportional reduction of
           congressional representation in any state that with-
           held suffrage from a portion of its adult male
           citizens
        C. 3, which disqualified Confederate officials from
           holding office in the restored Union
        D. 4, which repudiated the Confederate debt

50. During the first year or two of the war, Confederate   50.____
    officers were generally of higher quality than Union
    officers, because
        A. the South benefited from a large number of graduates
           from military academies
        B. Confederate officers were often trained by foreign
           officers
        C. officers in the South were generally from the upper
           class and, therefore, more literate
        D. they earned their position solely on the basis of
           performance in battle

KEY (CORRECT ANSWERS)

1. C	11. B	21. A	31. C	41. A
2. C	12. C	22. D	32. B	42. B
3. B	13. C	23. D	33. B	43. A
4. D	14. D	24. A	34. C	44. C
5. B	15. A	25. B	35. C	45. D
6. D	16. D	26. B	36. D	46. A
7. B	17. B	27. D	37. B	47. C
8. D	18. C	28. C	38. D	48. D
9. D	19. C	29. B	39. D	49. A
10. C	20. B	30. A	40. C	50. A

EXAMINATION SECTION
TEST 1

DIRECTIONS: Each question or incomplete statement is followed by several suggested answers or completions. Select the one that BEST answers the question or completes the statement. *PRINT THE LETTER OF THE CORRECT ANSWER IN THE SPACE AT THE RIGHT.*

1. As a result of the Missouri Compromise,   1.___
   A. Missouri was admitted to the Union as a free state
   B. slavery was prohibited in all of the Louisiana Territory
   C. Maine was admitted to the Union as a free state
   D. all of the Louisiana Territory was open to slavery

2. William Lloyd Garrison based his opposition to slavery on   2.___
   the belief that it was
   A. economically unsound   B. unconstitutional
   C. communistic in nature   D. morally wrong

3. In 1831, a slave uprising in Virginia was led by   3.___
   A. John Brown   B. Joseph Coxey
   C. Nat Turner   D. Daniel Shays

4. The Liberty Party was formed by people who favored   4.___
   A. women's suffrage
   B. temperance in drinking
   C. the abolition of slavery
   D. restrictions on immigration

5. A new interest in western expansion developed in the   5.___
   early 1800's out of
   A. a world-wide depression originating in western Europe
   B. overcrowded conditions in the East
   C. the need of southern planters to find land open to
      slavery
   D. a desire to spread Christianity to the Indians

6. The loudest protests against the annexation of Texas came   6.___
   from the
   A. expansionists   B. Southern planters
   C. abolitionists   D. New England industrialists

7. Mexico broke diplomatic relations with the United States   7.___
   in 1845 as a protest against
   A. American settlement of New Mexico
   B. the annexation of Texas
   C. the presence of the United States Navy off the
      California coast
   D. the stationing of American troops south of the Rio
      Grande River

8. The American drive on Mexico City in 1847 was led by   8.____
   General
   A. Zachary Taylor   B. Stephen W. Kearny
   C. J.D. Sloat   D. Winfield Scott

9. The FIRST of the territories ceded by Mexico after the   9.____
   Mexican War to gain a large enough population to request
   statehood was
   A. California   B. New Mexico
   C. Arizona   D. Nevada

10. The Free Soil Party   10.____
    A. made no stand on the issue of slavery
    B. was composed mainly of slave owners
    C. called for the abolition of slavery
    D. opposed the extension of slavery into the territories

11. According to the principle of popular sovereignty,   11.____
    A. the Missouri Compromise line was to be extended to
       the Pacific Ocean
    B. slavery was to be prohibited in all of the territory
       gained from Mexico
    C. the people who lived in each territory were to decide
       whether or not slavery was to be permitted there
    D. slavery and involuntary servitude were to be
       abolished wherever they existed

12. The important provisions of the Compromise of 1850 came 12.____
    from a series of measures presented to the Senate by
    A. William H. Seward   B. John C. Calhoun
    C. Henry Clay   D. Jefferson Davis

13. The Kansas-Nebraska Bill was pushed through both houses 13.____
    of Congress under the masterful leadership of
    A. Stephen A. Douglas   B. Daniel Webster
    C. Salmon P. Chase   D. Millard Filmore

14. The Republican Party was formed in   14.____
    A. 1854   B. 1856   C. 1858   D. 1860

15. The MOST dramatic change in American agriculture began 15.____
    in 1793 with the invention of the
    A. McCormick reaper   B. cotton gin
    C. mowing machine   D. combine

16. The incident which finally caused the southern states to 16.____
    secede from the Union was
    A. the passage of the Kansas-Nebraska Bill
    B. John Brown's raid of Harper's Ferry
    C. the election of Abraham Lincoln
    D. the Dred Scott decision

17. The Constitution of the Confederate States of America   17.___
    A. legalized the foreign slave trade
    B. provided for a protective tariff
    C. was completely different from the Constitution of
       the United States
    D. openly accepted the doctrine of state sovereignty

18. Four of the eight border states remained loyal to the   18.___
    Union during the Civil War: Delaware, Maryland, Kentucky,
    and
    A. Arkansas   B. Tennessee
    C. Missouri   D. North Carolina

19. The secession of Virginia in 1861   19.___
    A. was responsible for the Confederate attack on Fort
       Sumter
    B. left the Union without a good harbor
    C. deprived the Union of the services of Robert E. Lee
    D. brought France into the war on the side of the
       Confederacy

20. The Union campaign in the East during the Civil War   20.___
    centered around efforts to
    A. divide the Confederacy in two sections
    B. seize the Confederate capital at Richmond, Virginia
    C. open the Mississippi River to northern commerce
    D. capture the important southern railroad centers in
       South Carolina

21. All of the Civil War was fought below the Mason-Dixon   21.___
    line with the *important* exception of the Battle of
    A. Gettysburg   B. Manassas
    C. Vicksburg   D. Antietam

22. An *important* advantage which the South had in the early   22.___
    part of the Civil War was
    A. superior industrial resources
    B. more manpower
    C. more able military leaders
    D. a better navy and merchant marine

23. The MAJOR shortcomings of General George B. McClellan,   23.___
    who was, for a time, commander of the Union forces in
    the East, was that he
    A. had no previous experience
    B. was over-cautious
    C. lacked organizational skill
    D. was not popular with his men

24. A naval expedition under David Farragut paved the way for   24.___
    the Union capture in 1862 of
    A. Shiloh   B. Richmond
    C. New Orleans   D. Chattanooga

25. The Confederate invasion of Maryland in September, 1862, was checked by the defeat of the southern forces at
    A. Vicksburg B. Fredericksburg
    C. Chancellorsville D. Antietam

25.___

26. After March 1864, the commander of the Union armies was
    A. A.E. Burnside B. Ulysses S. Grant
    C. Joseph Hooker D. George G. Meade

26.___

27. The Union blockade of southern ports
    A. was very ineffective
    B. proved to be one of the most effective forces in overpowering the South
    C. had to be discontinued after 1862 because of a lack of Union ships
    D. was solely responsible for Lee's surrender at Appomatox

27.___

28. The battle of the Merrimac and the Monitor proved the
    A. superiority of the Union navy
    B. superiority of ironclad ships
    C. inefficiency of ironclad ships
    D. superiority of the Southern navy

28.___

29. The *Trent* incident of 1861 strained relations between the North and
    A. France B. Spain
    C. Great Britain D. Mexico

29.___

30. Great Britain and France
    A. favored the North through all of the Civil War
    B. became allies of the South early in the Civil War
    C. did not formally recognize the Confederacy
    D. provided the ships which the Union used in the blockade of southern ports

30.___

31. The Emancipation Proclamation
    A. offered a complete and final solution to the problem of slavery
    B. paved the way for a change in the Constitution that would legally abolish slavery
    C. applied to all states below the Mason-Dixon line
    D. was announced by Abraham Lincoln in his second inaugural address

31.___

32. The Copperheads were
    A. Republicans who favored the renomination of Abraham Lincoln in 1864
    B. Northerners who went south following the Civil War
    C. members of the Union Party
    D. extreme Democrats who called the Civil War a failure and urged immediate efforts to end it

32.___

33. Abraham Lincoln based his plan for southern reconstruction   33.____
    on his
    A. pardoning power
    B. veto power
    C. position as commander-in-chief of the armed forces
    D. power to appoint government officials

34. Andrew Johnson's plan for southern reconstruction was   34.____
    A. almost as generous as the Lincoln plan
    B. entirely different from the Lincoln plan
    C. very similar to the Congressional plan
    D. approved by Congress in 1865

35. The publisher of THE LIBERATOR, a newspaper which worked   35.____
    for the abolition of slavery, was
    A. Samuel G. Howe   B. Henry Ward Beecher
    C. William Lloyd Garrison   D. Harriet Beecher Stowe

36. Texas was NOT annexed by the United States until nearly   36.____
    ten years after she won her independence because
    A. most Texans wanted to remain an independent republic
    B. many Americans violently objected to admitting Texas
       into the Union
    C. President James Polk opposed annexation
    D. there was no legal way by which Texas could be
       annexed

37. The war with Mexico began when Mexican forces crossed the   37.____
    Rio Grande River and attacked a detachment of Americans
    led by
    A. Zachary Taylor   B. Robert E. Lee
    C. Andrew Jackson   D. William Henry Harrison

38. According to the terms of the Missouri Compromise,   38.____
    A. slavery was to be allowed in all of the Louisiana
       Territory
    B. Missouri was admitted to the Union as a slave state
    C. slavery was illegal in all of the Louisiana Territory
    D. Missouri was admitted to the Union as a free state

39. The idea that the United States government should keep   39.____
    its hands off all matters over which it had NOT been
    given definite authority by the Constitution became the
    basis for what is known as the doctrine of
    A. states' rights   B. mercantilism
    C. squatter sovereignty   D. federalism

40. In 1846, a provision that slavery should NEVER exist in   40.____
    any lands gained from Mexico was presented to Congress by
    A. John C. Calhoun   B. David Wilmot
    C. Daniel Webster   D. Robert Hayne

41. California was admitted to the Union as a free state under the terms of the
    A. Compromise of 1850   B. Kansas-Nebraska Bill
    C. Missouri Compromise   D. Great Compromise

41.___

42. Northern opinion *against* slavery was inflamed by UNCLE TOM'S CABIN, which was written by
    A. William Lloyd Garrison   B. Harriet Beecher Stowe
    C. James Waldo Emerson   D. Dorothea Dix

42.___

43. The people of the territories were allowed to decide whether or not they wanted to have slavery by the
    A. Dred Scott Decision   B. Kansas-Nebraska Act
    C. Compromise of 1820   D. Wilmot Proviso

43.___

44. In 1858, Abraham Lincoln engaged in a series of debates about slavery with
    A. Daniel Webster   B. Stephen A. Douglas
    C. James Buchanan   D. John C. Fremont

44.___

45. In 1859, John Brown led a group of men in an attack against the United States Armory at
    A. Sutter's Mill   B. Fort Sumter
    C. Harper's Ferry   D. Fort McHenry

45.___

46. The President of the Confederate States of America was
    A. John C. Breckinridge   B. Robert E. Lee
    C. William Seward   D. Jefferson Davis

46.___

47. Among the slave states that did NOT leave the Union at the beginning of the Civil War was
    A. Virginia   B. Arkansas   C. Tennessee   D. Missouri

47.___

48. The strategy of the South in the Civil War consisted largely of
    A. dividing the North into two separate sections
    B. capturing Washington, D.C. and other key northern cities
    C. holding out until the people of the North grew tired of the War
    D. blockading all northern ports

48.___

49. The North gained control of the Mississippi River in 1863 with the capture of Port Hudson and
    A. Vicksburg   B. Chattanooga
    C. Shiloh   D. Richmond

49.___

50. The naval battle between the ironclad ships Merrimac and Monitor ended
    A. in a draw
    B. when the Union Monitor was sunk
    C. when both ships were severely damaged
    D. with the destruction of the Confederate Merrimac

50.___

KEY (CORRECT ANSWERS)

1. C	11. C	21. A	31. B	41. A
2. D	12. C	22. C	32. D	42. B
3. C	13. A	23. B	33. A	43. C
4. C	14. A	24. C	34. A	44. B
5. C	15. B	25. D	35. C	45. C
6. C	16. C	26. B	36. B	46. D
7. B	17. D	27. B	37. A	47. D
8. D	18. C	28. B	38. B	48. C
9. A	19. C	29. C	39. A	49. A
10. D	20. B	30. C	40. B	50. A

TEST 2

DIRECTIONS: Each question or incomplete statement is followed by several suggested answers or completions. Select the one that BEST answers the question or completes the statement. *PRINT THE LETTER OF THE CORRECT ANSWER IN THE SPACE AT THE RIGHT.*

1. In the spring of 1862, an attempt to capture the Confederate capital at Richmond was made by Union forces led by
   A. George B. McClellan   B. *Stonewall* Jackson
   C. Ulysses S. Grant   D. William T. Sherman

   1.___

2. The Civil War ended in
   A. 1863   B. 1864   C. 1865   D. 1866

   2.___

3. Abraham Lincoln was assassinated by
   A. John Wilkes Booth   B. Aaron Burr
   C. Alexander Stephens   D. William H. Seward

   3.___

4. The Vice President who became President upon the death of Abraham Lincoln was
   A. Andrew Johnson   B. Ulysses S. Grant
   C. James Buchanan   D. Zachary Taylor

   4.___

5. The Missouri Compromise of 1820
   A. prohibited slavery in all of the Louisiana Territory
   B. permitted settlers in a territory to decide the issue of slavery
   C. brought a permanent end to sectional self-consciousness between the North and the South
   D. maintained the balance between slave states and free states

   5.___

6. In order to keep producing large quantities of cotton, southern planters
   A. employed scientific methods
   B. gradually gave up slave labor
   C. kept looking for new lands
   D. reduced the size of most plantations

   6.___

7. The progress of industry in America was *greatly* aided by the increased use of
   A. slave labor   B. home manufacturing
   C. government controls   D. steam power

   7.___

8. The American or *Know-Nothing* Party of the mid-1800's was a semi-secret political organization opposed to
   A. big business   B. immigrants
   C. westward expansion   D. woman suffrage

   8.___

9. In MOST cases, slaves in the South received fairly good   9.___
   treatment because
   A. there were strict laws against mistreating them
   B. they were ALWAYS willing and energetic workers
   C. the federal government outlined strict rules for slave
      owners
   D. they were valuable property and represented a heavy
      investment

10. Northern abolitionists helped runaway slaves to escape by   10.___
    using the
    A. Fugitive Slave Law   B. *liberty express*
    C. *underground railroad*   D. American System

11. Early in the 1800's, a new interest in westward expansion   11.___
    grew out of
    A. the needs of southern cotton growers
    B. a demand for more and better beef cattle
    C. a shortage of wheat on the world market
    D. a severe depression in the industrial Northeast

12. The war for the independence of Texas broke out as a   12.___
    result of
    A. the invasion of Mexico by Spanish forces
    B. severe restrictions placed on the Texans by the
       Mexican government
    C. the activities of an American force commanded by
       Zachary Taylor
    D. an attempt by France to establish a dictatorship in
       Mexico

13. The war for Texan independence was decided by the defeat   13.___
    of Mexican forces at the battle of
    A. San Jacinto   B. the Alamo
    C. Goliad   D. San Antonio

14. The Presidential election of 1844 was won by the Democratic 14.___
    candidate who *strongly* favored annexation and expansion:
    A. Martin Van Buren   B. John Tyler
    C. Zachary Taylor   D. James Polk

15. The Mexican War ended with the signing of the Treaty of   15.___
    A. Ghent   B. Monterrey
    C. Guadalupe-Hidalgo   D. Paris

16. The Wilmot Proviso was   16.___
    A. generally condemned in the North
    B. defeated by the Senate each time a vote was taken
    C. popular in the slave states
    D. passed by Congress over the veto of the President

17. The author of noninterference with slavery in the   17.___
    territories was
    A. Stephen A. Douglas   B. Abraham Lincoln
    C. John C. Calhoun   D. John C. Fremont

18. The Kansas-Nebraska Bill was   18.___
    A. favored by southern congressmen
    B. vigorously attacked in the South
    C. popular with anti-slavery forces
    D. part of the Missouri Compromise

19. The Supreme Court decision in the case of Dred Scott was   19.___
    written by Chief Justice
    A. Roger Taney   B. John Marshall
    C. Daniel Webster   D. John Jay

20. In effect, the Dred Scott decision meant that   20.___
    A. Congress had no power to regulate slavery in the
       territories
    B. the Kansas-Nebraska Act was unconstitutional
    C. slaves were no longer considered the property of
       their owners
    D. the Missouri Compromise was the best means of stopping
       the spread of slavery

21. In his inaugural address, Abraham Lincoln denied any   21.___
    intention of
    A. trying to enforce Union laws in the South
    B. collecting federal duties and taxes in the South
    C. interfering with slavery in the states where it
       legally existed
    D. allowing a Civil War to occur

22. The term *border states* refers to the states that   22.___
    A. lay between the North and the cotton states
    B. formed the southern boundary of the Confederacy
    C. lay between the United States and the frontier
    D. were affected by the Union blockade

23. The FIRST of the southern states to secede from the Union 23.___
    was
    A. Georgia   B. South Carolina
    C. Texas   D. Kentucky

24. The credit for the success of the Union   campaign in the 24.___
    West belongs to
    A. *Stonewall* Jackson B. George B. McClellan
    C. Joseph E. Johnston   D. Ulysses S. Grant

25. During the years 1861-63, the Union forces in the East   25.___
    A. had little success
    B. succeeded in capturing Richmond
    C. did not allow any invasions of Union territory
    D. defeated Confederate forces at Manassas Junction and
       Bull Run

26. The terms of surrender which General Grant offered to   26.___
    General Lee at Appomattox were
    A. very harsh
    B. turned down by the Confederacy
    C. very generous
    D. later approved by Congress

27. The need to break the Union blockade led the Confederacy   27.___
    to experiment with
    A. ocean-going steamboats   B. packet ships
    C. clipper ships   D. ironclad ships

28. Perhaps the MOST surprising part of the Civil War was that   28.___
    the
    A. Union was able to enforce the blockade
    B. Confederacy was able to hold out until 1865
    C. Confederacy collapsed as soon as it did
    D. South was able to negotiate treaties with England
       and France

29. The CHIEF method used by the South to finance the Civil   29.___
    War was
    A. paper money   B. an income tax
    C. foreign loans   D. the sale of war bonds

30. *Fourscore and seven years ago* are the opening words of   30.___
    A. the Gettysburg Address
    B. Lincoln's Second Inaugural Address
    C. the Emancipation Proclamation
    D. the Constitution of the Confederate States of America

31. Slavery in the United States was prohibited by the   31.___
    A. Emancipation Proclamation
    B. Thirteenth Amendment
    C. Fourteenth Amendment
    D. Fifteenth Amendment

32. The MOST outspoken of the Democrats who opposed the   32.___
    re-election of Abraham Lincoln in 1864 were called
    A. Carpetbaggers   B. Scalawags
    C. Muckrackers   D. Copperheads

33. Under the pressure of war needs, industry in the North   33.___
    A. increased
    B. decreased
    C. felt a severe manpower shortage
    D. suffered a severe depression

34. Abraham Lincoln's plans for southern reconstruction were   34.___
    A. adopted by Congress
    B. charitable and humane
    C. based on the *state suicide* theory
    D. carried out after his death

35. Abraham Lincoln was assassinated in April,   35.___
    A. 1863   B. 1864   C. 1865   D. 1866

36. During the Civil War, the Monroe Doctrine was challenged   36.___
    by the establishment of a puppet ruler in Mexico by
    A. Great Britain   B. France
    C. Germany   D. Spain

37. A policy of free western land was established with the   37.___
    passage in 1862 of the
    A. Land Ordinance   B. Homestead Act
    C. Morrill Act   D. Northwest Ordinance

38. Paper money WITHOUT specific backing issued by the Federal   38.___
    government to finance the Civil War was called
    A. hard money   B. free silver
    C. greenbacks   D. bonds

39. Hinton R. Helper's THE IMPENDING CRISIS OF THE SOUTH   39.___
    attempted to prove that in the South slavery had the
    WORST effect on
    A. families of wealthy slave owners
    B. owners of fewer than ten slaves
    C. the middle class
    D. non-slaveholding whites

40. Which one of the following statements applies to the South   40.___
    during the Reconstruction Era?
    A. Control of the southern economy by the plantation
       aristocracy was shattered.
    B. The Democratic Party maintained control of the Senate
       despite Radical Republican control in the House of
       Representatives.
    C. The Ku Klux Klan dominated southern state legislatures.
    D. The *black codes* were enacted to protect the voting
       rights of Negroes.

41. Which one of the following was a BASIC reason for the   41.___
    passage of the Fifteenth Amendment?
    The
    A. Supreme Court's decision that the Civil Rights Act
       of 1866 was unconstitutional
    B. desire to assure the Negro's permanent status as a
       free man by replacing the Emancipation Proclamation
       with an amendment
    C. conviction of many Radical Republicans that penalties
       provided by the Fourteenth Amendment for disfran-
       chising the Negro were inadequate
    D. general feeling throughout the nation that Negro
       advances warranted such a step

42. Which one of the following events MOST immediately pre-   42.___
    ceded the end of the Reconstruction period in the South?
    The
    A. second inauguration of Ulysses S. Grant as President
    B. adoption of the Fourteenth Amendment
    C. election of Rutherford B. Hayes as President
    D. impeachment of Andrew Johnson

43. The demand for *resumption* in the 1870's was a demand that   43.___
    the United States government restore the
    A. gold standard
    B. unlimited coinage of silver
    C. issuance of greenbacks
    D. redemption of paper currency with metallic money on
        demand

44. The issue over which the Republican and Democratic parties   44.___
    differed MOST sharply in the three decades after the Civil
    War was
    A. tariff   B. imperialism
    C. railroad regulation   D. banking reform

45. In what respect was the situation of the American farmer   45.___
    in the 1920's different from that of the American farmer
    in the period 1865-1900?
    He
    A. faced foreign competition because of the expansion
        of agricultural production in Canada, Latin America,
        Australia, and Europe
    B. faced a decline in American exports of food and
        other farm products
    C. had inadequate credit facilities and high interest
        charges
    D. bought supplies and equipment in a protected market
        and sold his crops in a competitive world market

46. During which one of the following decades was there the   46.___
    LEAST resistance to Negro participation in government
    by the existing state governments in the South?
    A. 1855-1865   B. 1865-1875
    C. 1900-1910   D. 1950-1960

47. In which one of the following respects was the period   47.___
    between 1850 and 1860 in the United States MOST different
    from the period between 1840 and 1850?
    A. Emphasis on the establishment of a national banking
        system
    B. Concern over federal regulation of interstate commerce
    C. Recurring crises over sectional issues
    D. Desire to abandon the policy of isolation

48. During the pre-Civil War period, MOST immigrants settled   48.___
    in the North and West because
    A. the South discouraged them by discriminatory legisla-
        tion
    B. they preferred small farms rather than the large
        plantation holdings of the South
    C. they could not compete with the slave labor of the
        South
    D. they encountered no discrimination in these regions

49. The Republican Party platform in 1860 contained a plank   49.___
    on slavery which advocated the
    A. abolition of slavery in all states and territories
       of the Union
    B. prohibition of expansion of slavery into the terri-
       tories
    C. emancipation of the slaves in areas where it existed
       with just compensation to owners
    D. emancipation of all slaves with provision for econo-
       mic assistance to the freed slaves

50. Which group was MOST likely to win the sympathy of   50.___
    Southerners during the middle decades of the nineteenth
    century?
    A. Copperheads   B. Carpetbaggers
    C. Liberal Party   D. Scalawags

___

KEY (CORRECT ANSWERS)

1. A	11. A	21. C	31. B	41. C
2. C	12. B	22. A	32. D	42. C
3. A	13. A	23. B	33. A	43. D
4. A	14. D	24. D	34. B	44. A
5. D	15. C	25. A	35. C	45. B
6. C	16. B	26. C	36. B	46. B
7. D	17. C	27. D	37. B	47. C
8. B	18. A	28. B	38. C	48. C
9. D	19. A	29. A	39. D	49. B
10. C	20. A	30. A	40. A	50. A

TEST 3

DIRECTIONS: Each question or incomplete statement is followed by several suggested answers or completions. Select the one that BEST answers the question or completes the statement. *PRINT THE LETTER OF THE CORRECT ANSWER IN THE SPACE AT THE RIGHT.*

1. The MOST popular method of travel in the United States from the east coast to the west coast during the period 1849-1869 was
   A. transcontinental railroad
   B. ship and wagon train via the isthmus of Panama
   C. ship around Cape Horn
   D. wagon train across the country

   1.___

2. Though Congress had levied a tax on personal incomes during the Civil War, the Supreme Court FIRST declared such a tax unconstitutional during President Cleveland's administration because the
   A. Civil War income tax law had been upheld as a war measure
   B. Civil War income tax law was never tested in the Supreme Court before it was repealed in 1873
   C. passage of an income tax law over President Cleveland's veto made a Supreme Court test obligatory
   D. Supreme Court was ineffectual during the Civil War and the years that followed

   2.___

3. Henry Clay's American system was designed to
   A. strengthen the political power of the West as against the East and South
   B. compromise differences between North and South on tariff legislation
   C. facilitate expansion to the Pacific coast
   D. reduce sectional differences by creation of a unified economy

   3.___

4. The traditional method of determining the expansion of slavery into new territories by Congressional enactments that defined its limits was abandoned in the case of the
   A. Northwest Territory   B. Louisiana Territory
   C. Mexican Cession   D. Oregon Territory

   4.___

5. Daniel Webster reversed his traditional stand in regard to states' rights in the
   A. Dartmouth College Case
   B. Webster-Hayne Debates
   C. debate on the Compromise of 1850
   D. Kansas-Nebraska Bill

   5.___

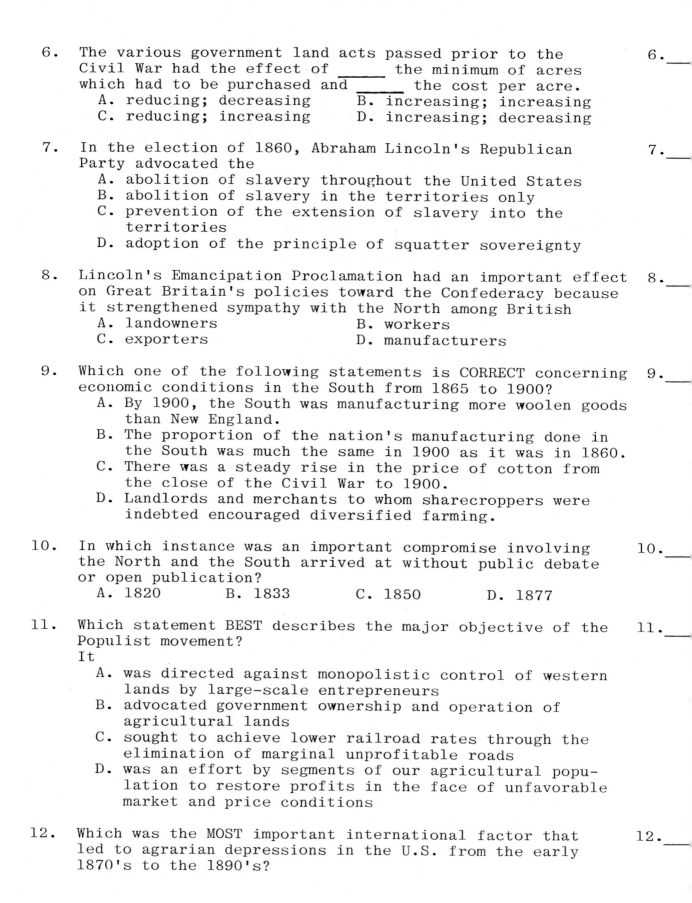

6. The various government land acts passed prior to the   6.___
   Civil War had the effect of _____ the minimum of acres
   which had to be purchased and _____ the cost per acre.
      A. reducing; decreasing   B. increasing; increasing
      C. reducing; increasing   D. increasing; decreasing

7. In the election of 1860, Abraham Lincoln's Republican   7.___
   Party advocated the
      A. abolition of slavery throughout the United States
      B. abolition of slavery in the territories only
      C. prevention of the extension of slavery into the
         territories
      D. adoption of the principle of squatter sovereignty

8. Lincoln's Emancipation Proclamation had an important effect 8.___
   on Great Britain's policies toward the Confederacy because
   it strengthened sympathy with the North among British
      A. landowners   B. workers
      C. exporters   D. manufacturers

9. Which one of the following statements is CORRECT concerning 9.___
   economic conditions in the South from 1865 to 1900?
      A. By 1900, the South was manufacturing more woolen goods
         than New England.
      B. The proportion of the nation's manufacturing done in
         the South was much the same in 1900 as it was in 1860.
      C. There was a steady rise in the price of cotton from
         the close of the Civil War to 1900.
      D. Landlords and merchants to whom sharecroppers were
         indebted encouraged diversified farming.

10. In which instance was an important compromise involving   10.___
    the North and the South arrived at without public debate
    or open publication?
       A. 1820   B. 1833   C. 1850   D. 1877

11. Which statement BEST describes the major objective of the 11.___
    Populist movement?
    It
       A. was directed against monopolistic control of western
          lands by large-scale entrepreneurs
       B. advocated government ownership and operation of
          agricultural lands
       C. sought to achieve lower railroad rates through the
          elimination of marginal unprofitable roads
       D. was an effort by segments of our agricultural popu-
          lation to restore profits in the face of unfavorable
          market and price conditions

12. Which was the MOST important international factor that   12.___
    led to agrarian depressions in the U.S. from the early
    1870's to the 1890's?

A. An almost uninterrupted international price decline
B. Japanese rise to power in the Far East
C. European wars
D. European emigration to America

13. All of the following factors helped bring about the
    annexation of Texas in 1845 EXCEPT:
    A. Texas was becoming a center of foreign intrigue
    B. Mexican officials finally recognized Texas' inde-
       pendence
    C. Americans were caught up in the fever of manifest
       destiny
    D. Annexation was an important campaign issue in the
       election of 1844   13.___

14. Which one of the following may NOT be included in a list
    of the influences of the *frontier* on American history?
    It
    A. acted as a possible *safety valve* for economic unrest
    B. retarded the development of the industrial East
    C. had a democratizing influence on the country
    D. was a spur at once to individual initiative and
       collective social action   14.___

15. Which one of the following men was MOST unlike the other
    three in his views regarding slavery?
    A. Wendell Phillips   B. Henry Ward Beecher
    C. Daniel Webster   D. John G. Whittier   15.___

16. The doctrine of popular sovereignty was FIRST stated in
    the
    A. Wilmot Proviso   B. Compromise of 1850
    C. Kansas-Nebraska Act   D. Missouri Compromise   16.___

17. Of the following, the TWO leading senators who made
    possible the passage of the Compromise of 1850 were
    A. Calhoun and Clay   B. Clay and Webster
    C. Clay and Douglas   D. Calhoun and Webster   17.___

18. Which one of the following was NOT a provision of the
    Compromise of 1850?
    A. A strict fugitive slave law
    B. Missouri to be admitted as a slave state
    C. Texas to be given ten million dollars for surrender-
       ing territory to the federal government
    D. California to be admitted as a free state   18.___

19. Which of the following did NOT represent a clash of
    interest between the United States and Great Britain
    during the Civil War?
    I. Trent Affair   II. Monitor v. Merrimac
    III. Alabama Raids   IV. Maximilian Affair   19.___

    The CORRECT answer is:
    A. I, IV   B. I, III   C. II, III   D. II, IV

20. Which one of the following reasons was NOT advanced by   20.___
the Radical Republicans who opposed the Lincoln-Johnson
plans for Reconstruction?
   A. They believed that southern leaders should be punished
by being stripped of civil rights and property.
   B. They wanted to restore the balance of power between
the executive and legislative branches of the government which had existed prior to the war.
   C. They feared that granting the ballot to the Negro
would drive Southern whites into the Democratic Party.
   D. Southern governments set up under the Lincoln-Johnson
plan were under the control of the Democratic Party.

21. Which of the following is NOT true regarding the 14th   21.___
Amendment?
It
   A. provided for a proportionate reduction in representa-
tion in the House when a state denied the franchise
   B. abrogated the *three-fifths* clause, thereby increasing
Southern representation in the House of Representa-
tives
   C. was formulated because of widespread doubt as to the
constitutionality of the Civil Rights Act
   D. honored the payment of both the Union and the
Confederate debt

22. Which one of the following promises was NOT made to   22.___
Southern Democratic leaders in return for their support
in the election of Hayes over Tilden?
The
   A. withdrawal of federal troops from the South
   B. appropriation by Congress of substantial funds for
internal improvements in the South
   C. downward revision of the high post-war tariffs
   D. appointment of at least one Southerner to the Cabinet

23. Which one of the following statements is NOT true concern-   23.___
ing the currency situation after the Civil War?
   A. At the close of the war, farmers urged that government
bonds be redeemable in greenbacks.
   B. In 1875, Congress provided for the redemption of
greenbacks by specie.
   C. In order to maintain purchasing power, businessmen
favored continuance of greenback currency.
   D. At his inauguration, President Grant favored redemption of government bonds in gold.

24. Which one of the following was NOT a factor responsible   24.___
for the rapid settlement of the Far West from 1870 to
1890?
   A. Transportation facilities
   B. Increased immigration
   C. Government soil conservation policies
   D. New methods of fencing

25. Which of the following statements does NOT describe an   25.___
    essential factor of the Economic Revolution (1865-1900)
    in the U.S.?
    The
    A. acquisition of a labor supply sufficiently large and
       cheap for the purposes of industry
    B. acquisition of colonies containing many valuable
       raw materials
    C. discovery and the exploitation of natural resources
       such as iron, coal, copper, oil
    D. growth of a domestic market and the development of
       foreign markets

26. Which of the following developments could be observed in   26.___
    education in the United States during the period from
    1865-1900?
    I. Educational facilities increased faster than popula-
       tion.
    II. Graduate studies were offered by an increasing number
        of universities.
    III. There was a growing interest in adult education and
         in library building.
    IV. The teaching profession achieved adequate standards
        throughout the nation.

    The CORRECT answer is:
    A. II, III, IV   B. I, II, III, IV
    C. I, II, III   D. I, III, IV

27. Which one of the following was NOT advocated by the   27.___
    American farmer between 1870-1890 in his attempt to solve
    his problems?
    A. Cooperative marketing of produce
    B. Government regulation of interstate carriers
    C. Contraction of the currency to raise prices
    D. Political action through the formation of third
       parties

28. Which group of states created from territories acquired   28.___
    before the Civil War was admitted to the Union after 1900?
    A. Oklahoma, New Mexico, Arizona
    B. Minnesota, Michigan, Wisconsin
    C. Washington, Oregon, Utah
    D. Nevada, Wyoming, Idaho

29. The purpose of Henry Clay's *American System* was to   29.___
    A. prevent the dissolution of the Union over the slavery
       issue
    B. isolate the United States from foreign entanglements
    C. unify the sections of the country by having the
       federal government meet their economic needs
    D. win the South from its allegiance to John Calhoun

30. Which one of the following was NOT a provision of the Omnibus Bill of 1850?
    A. A stricter fugitive slave law was to be enacted
    B. Adjustment of the Texas-New Mexico boundary
    C. Slavery was to be prohibited in the District of Columbia
    D. California was to be admitted as a free state

30.___

31. Which one of the following was NOT part of the platform of the Republican Party in the Presidential Campaign of 1860?
    A. Support of local option with regard to the question of slavery in the territories
    B. No interference with slavery in the states
    C. Support of the protective tariff
    D. Promise of free public land to settlers

31.___

32. Which one of the following statements is NOT true of the *New South* after the Civil War?
    A. The agricultural revolution touched the South less than any other section of the country.
    B. Though farms were smaller, farm tenancy was more widespread.
    C. The most striking difference between the *New South* and the *Old South* was the rise of industry and manufacturers.
    D. Since immigration avoided the South, there was a severe shortage of cheap labor.

32.___

33. Which one of the following statements would NOT correctly apply to the West after the Civil War?
    A. The generation after the Civil War witnessed the most extensive movement of population in our history.
    B. Many new states with a taste for social and political experiments arose in the West.
    C. The region of the Great Plains was one in which Eastern farming methods could best be applied.
    D. The Plains environment necessitated a modification of social attitudes and of political and legal institutions.

33.___

34. Which of the following statements would NOT appear in a chapter in a textbook on American history entitled, *The Economic Revolution - 1865-1900*?
    A. It was the dream of Jefferson that his country was to be a great agrarian democracy.
    B. The U.S. was progressing in the direction of a diversified, self-sufficing nation, as advocated by Hamilton.
    C. Spokesmen of big business were appealing for Hamilton's interpretation of the Constitution as against Jefferson's.
    D. Within two generations of Jefferson's death, the value of American manufactured products was almost triple that of the agricultural.

34.___

35. Which of the following was NOT a reason for the general   35.___
    expansion of U.S. agriculture after 1860?
    A. Lack of competition in world markets from other
       countries
    B. Opening up of new agricultural land
    C. Growth of population
    D. Improved transportation facilities

36. Which of the following was NOT an issue on which Daniel   36.___
    Webster took a prominent position?
    The
    A. Compact Theory
    B. Compromise of 1850
    C. Dartmouth College Charter
    D. Yazoo land claims

37. Which one of the following pairs expressed a similar   37.___
    purpose or principle concerning the slavery issue?
    A. Northwest Ordinance - Compromise of 1850
    B. Missouri Compromise - Kansas-Nebraska Act
    C. Dred Scott Decision - Freeport Doctrine
    D. Free Soil Party - Republican Party (1854-1860)

38. Which of the following statements BEST explains England's   38.___
    neutrality in the American Civil War?
      I. The effect of the Emancipation Proclamation
     II. Dependence on Northern exports of wheat
    III. The democratic attitudes in the English government
     IV. The surpluses of Egyptian cotton
      V. English war profits

    The CORRECT answer is:
      A. I, II, IV   B. III, IV, V
      C. I, IV, V   D. I, II, V

39. The pair which does NOT represent a cause and effect   39.___
    relationship is
    A. Tenure of Office Act - Impeachment of Andrew Johnson
    B. National Banking Acts - Establishment of the Indepen-
       dent Treasury System
    C. Black codes - Civil Rights Bill
    D. Ku Klux Klan - Force Acts (1870-1871)

40. Which of the following may be CORRECTLY considered as   40.___
    contributing to the rapid development of the West between
    1865 and 1900?
      I. Federal government's liberal land grants
     II. High prices offered for farm products
    III. Marked increase in migration from Europe
     IV. Protection of the farmers' market through tariff
         legislation

    The CORRECT answer is:
      A. I, III   B. II, IV   C. I, IV   D. II, III

41. In connection with the slavery issue, the *gag rule* was   41.____
    fought on the floor of Congress in the 1830's by
        A. Henry Clay   B. William Lloyd Garrison
        C. John Quincy Adams   D. James G. Birney

42. On which one of the following policies were Clay and   42.____
    Calhoun LEAST in harmony?
        A. Declaration of war on England in 1812
        B. Tariff of 1816
        C. Chartering the Second Bank of the United States
        D. Election of John Quincy Adams

43. The two men who were MOST in agreement in the debate on   43.____
    the Compromise of 1850 were
        A. Clay and Calhoun   B. Calhoun and Webster
        C. Clay and Webster   D. Seward and Webster

44. Which of the following were considered by Southerners to   44.____
    be attacks on slavery?
        I. Tallmadge Amendment   II. Wilmot Proviso
      III. Ostend Manifesto   IV. *The Impending Crisis*
        A. II,III,IV   B. I,III,IV   C. I,II,III   D. I,II,IV

45. What is the CORRECT chronological order of the following   45.____
    events?
        I. John Brown's raid
       II. Dred Scott decision
      III. Lincoln-Douglas debates
       IV. Founding of the Republican Party

    The CORRECT answer is:
        A. II, IV, III, I   B. III, II, I, IV
        C. IV, III, II, I   D. IV, II, III, I

46. Which statement is CORRECT in regard to the Kansas-   46.____
    Nebraska Act?
    It
        A. made Kansas free and Nebraska slave
        B. repealed the Missouri Compromise
        C. admitted Kansas as a slave state
        D. repealed the Compromise of 1850

47. Which of the following is TRUE of the election of 1850?   47.____
        A. Lincoln obtained a large popular majority.
        B. Republicans were a minority in each house of Congress.
        C. Douglas lost practically all the Southern popular
           vote to Breckinridge.
        D. Lincoln was elected by a narrow majority of electoral
           votes.

48. During the American Civil War, England   48.____
        A. refrained from declaring her neutrality
        B. recognized the independence of the Confederacy
        C. recognized the Confederacy as a belligerent
        D. obtained sufficient cotton from the South to keep
           its factories going

49. The opponent of Lincoln in the election of 1864 was   49.___
    A. Fremont   B. McClellan C. Greeley   D. Stanton

50. A famous case in the Civil War period in which the Supreme   50.___
    Court held that neither the President nor Congress could
    declare martial law in places where civil courts were open
    was
       A. Mississippi vs. Johnson B. ex parte Milligan
       C. Georgia vs. Stanton   D. ex parte McCardle

—

KEY (CORRECT ANSWERS)

1. C	11. D	21. D	31. A	41. C
2. B	12. A	22. C	32. D	42. D
3. D	13. B	23. C	33. C	43. C
4. C	14. B	24. C	34. C	44. D
5. C	15. C	25. B	35. A	45. D
6. A	16. B	26. C	36. D	46. B
7. C	17. B	27. C	37. D	47. B
8. B	18. B	28. A	38. D	48. C
9. B	19. D	29. C	39. B	49. B
10. D	20. C	30. C	40. A	50. B

—

TEST 4

DIRECTIONS: Each question or incomplete statement is followed by several suggested answers or completions. Select the one that BEST answers the question or completes the statement. *PRINT THE LETTER OF THE CORRECT ANSWER IN THE SPACE AT THE RIGHT.*

1. An excellent example of the Supreme Court's refusal to increase the power of the central government at the expense of state governments in the field of regulating business is
   A. Gibbons vs. Ogden, 1824
   B. Slaughter House cases, 1873
   C. Wabash vs. Illinois, 1886
   D. Pollock vs. Farmers Loan and Trust Company, 1895

   1.___

2. The MOST valuable form of aid given by the Federal government to railroads in the period after the Civil War was
   A. land grants   B. loans
   C. subsidies   D. tariff remission on rails

   2.___

3. Which one of the following may CORRECTLY be considered a result of the influence of the other three?
   The
   A. influx of large numbers of immigrants
   B. rise of big business
   C. urbanization of American life
   D. increased mechanization of agriculture

   3.___

4. Which one of the following BEST states a principle established by the Dred Scott decision?
   A. Congress could abolish slavery in the territories.
   B. Congress could not legislate concerning slavery in the territories.
   C. Slaves residing in free territory automatically gained freedom.
   D. The territories, through popular sovereignty, had the sole right to decide the question of slavery within their limits.

   4.___

5. Which one of the following boundary disputes was settled in a manner DIFFERENT from the others?
   _____ boundary.
   A. Maine   B. Oregon
   C. Texan   D. Louisiana Territory

   5.___

6. Which one of the following terms has been used to characterize the social and cultural life in the United States during the period 1870-1900?
   The
   A. Tragic Era   B. Age of Hate
   C. New Freedom   D. Gilded Age

   6.___

7. The 19th century American statesman who was the leading   7.___
   proponent of the theory of the concurrent minority, which
   guaranteed to large economic interests and geographic
   units a veto on the majority determination was
     A. John C. Calhoun   B. Henry Clay
     C. Stephen A. Douglas   D. Daniel Webster

8. Which one of the following permitted settlers in the   8.___
   Louisiana Territory to decide the question of slavery
   for themselves?
   The
     A. Dred Scott Decision   B. Missouri Compromise
     C. Wilmot Proviso   D. Kansas-Nebraska Act

9. Lincoln's Emancipation Proclamation   9.___
     A. contained a forceful indictment of slavery
     B. was based on military necessity
     C. declared all slaves in all the slave states to be free
     D. was issued after a succession of military victories
        by the North

10. The years immediately following the Civil War were   10.___
    similar to the years immediately following the War of
    1812 because in both periods
      A. the executive and legislative branches were con-
         trolled by different parties
      B. the legislatures were unable to pass necessary laws
      C. the Presidents were successful military leaders but
         unsuccessful in civil office
      D. for practical purposes, no effective opposition
         groups operated in Congress

11. One of the arguments used by those who favored high   11.___
    tariff rates following the Civil War was that high
    tariffs would
      A. promote a greater volume of world trade
      B. encourage the development of new industries
      C. stop the growth of huge industrial combinations
      D. keep prices and wages low

12. The Missouri Compromise (1820), the Compromise of 1850,   12.___
    and the Kansas-Nebraska Act (1854)
      A. were a series of laws passed by Congress
      B. concerned the status of slavery in the Western terri-
         tories
      C. dealt with sectional disputes which finally led to
         civil war
      D. all of the above

Questions 13-14.

DIRECTIONS: Questions 13 and 14 refer to the following chart.

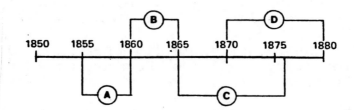

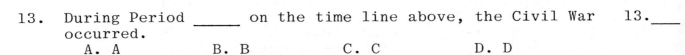

13. During Period _____ on the time line above, the Civil War   13.___
    occurred.
       A. A   B. B   C. C   D. D

14. The Reconstruction Era *generally* refers to Period _____   14.___
    on the time line above.
       A. A   B. B   C. C   D. D

15.   15.___

    Which of the territory areas above did Mexico cede to the
    United States after losing the Mexican War?
       A. A   B. B   C. C   D. D

16. The invention of new farm machinery after 1850 contributed   16.___
    to
       A. the growth of New York as a manufacturing city
       B. the introduction of several new crops
       C. an increase in the size of farms
       D. a decline in farm production

17. The strategy of the North for winning the Civil War was to   17.___
       A. hold out until the South tired of war
       B. gain foreign aid
       C. conquer by dividing the Confederacy in two
       D. capture General Lee

18. From the end of the Civil War until 1900, the pace of   18.___
    industrial change in the United States
       A. grew faster and faster
       B. was unchecked by panics or depressions
       C. remained relatively slow
       D. was halted by the growth of labor unions

19. The spectacular growth of industry following the Civil   19.___
    War was
       A. limited almost entirely to the Northeast
       B. not evident in the Midwest
       C. not confined to any one section of the country
       D. based on a very unstable foundation

20. The FALSE statement about the Northwest Ordinance is that   20.___
    it
       A. was a law which told how U.S. territories should be
          governed
       B. told how new states would be admitted to the Union
       C. guaranteed the personal liberties of people living
          in the territories
       D. told how states could peacefully leave the Union

21. The Battle of Gettysburg was considered a MAJOR turning   21.___
    point in the
       A. Revolutionary War   B. War of 1812
       C. Civil War   D. Spanish-American War

22. Which invention had the GREATEST impact upon the political   22.___
    institutions of nineteenth-century America?
       A. Airplane   B. Atomic bomb
       C. Cotton gin   D. Automobile

Question 23.

DIRECTIONS: Question 23 is based on the following passage.

*Convinced that the old parties had only tried to sidestep the
burning issue of the day, they believed that the time had come to
organize a new party. By joining with the Free-Soilers party,
they were confident that they could march to victory in 1856 or
certainly in 1860.*

23. The *burning* issue which had been sidestepped was   23.___
       A. free and unlimited coinage of silver
       B. the extension of slavery into the territories
       C. the annexation of Oregon
       D. civil service reform

24. By _____, Congress started a great tide of westward   24.___
    migration.
       A. placing Indians on reservations
       B. passing the Reconstruction Acts
       C. promoting soil conservation
       D. passing the Homestead Act

25. The Missouri Compromise was dead and a new act, which   25.___
    would let the territories decide for themselves whether
    to be slave or free, would take its place.
    The basic principle of this new act is called
        A. states' rights   B. direct democracy
        C. Manifest Destiny   D. popular sovereignty

Question 26.

DIRECTIONS: Question 26 shows a newspaper headline from the first
             half of the nineteenth century. Decide which man's
             actions might have led to that headline.

26. VICE PRESIDENT CHARGES THAT NEW TARIFF BENEFITS NEW   26.___
    ENGLAND FACTORY OWNERS AT EXPENSE OF SOUTHERN PLANTERS
    AND WESTERN FARMERS
        A. Henry Clay   B. Andrew Jackson
        C. Daniel Webster   D. John C. Calhoun

27. America's emergence as a MAJOR industrial country occurred   27.___
    between
        A. the War of 1812 and the Mexican War
        B. the Mexican War and the Civil War
        C. the Civil War and World War I
        D. World War I and World War II

28. From 1860 until 1885, national politics in the United   28.___
    States were controlled by the _____ Party.
        A. Progressive   B. Democrat
        C. Republican   D. Whig

29. The gold conspiracy of 1869 was due, in part, to the   29.___
    over-trusting nature of President
        A. Andrew Johnson   B. Ulysses S. Grant
        C. Rutherford B. Hayes   D. James A. Garfield

30. In the election of 1872, Ulysses S. Grant was opposed by   30.___
    New York editor
        A. Horace Greeley   B. Samuel J. Tilden
        C. Jay Gould   D. William Lloyd Garrison

31. The disputed election of 1876 was settled by   31.___
        A. an Electoral Commission
        B. the Supreme Court
        C. the Electoral College
        D. the House of Representatives

32. In the politics of the decade after the Civil War, the   32.___
    issue of slavery focused on whether
        A. racial equality should be the foremost national
           priority
        B. slavery should be permitted to exist in the terri-
           tories

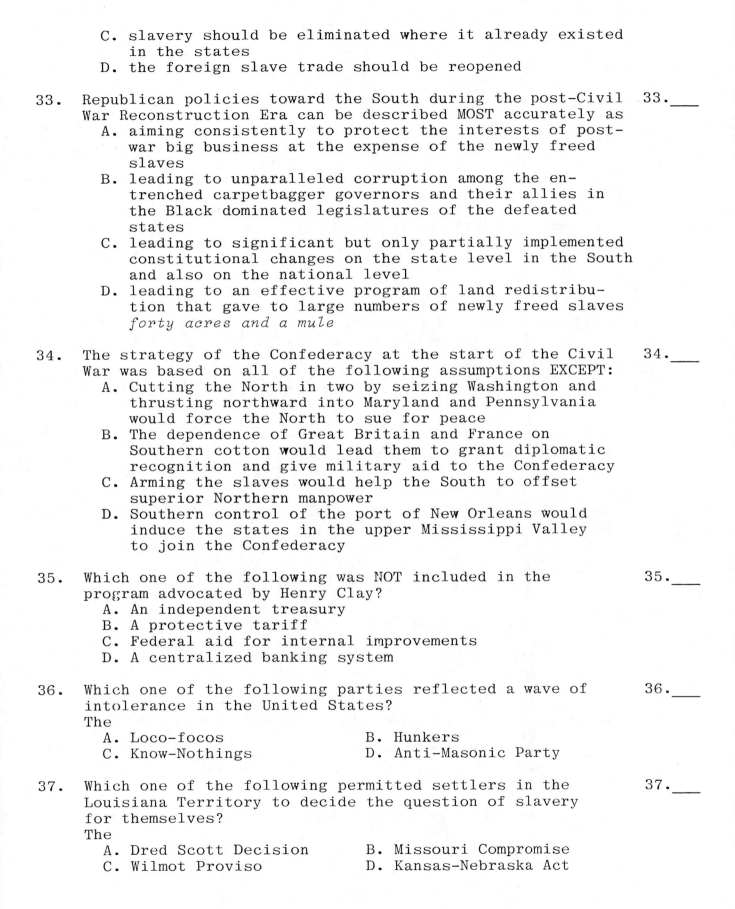

C. slavery should be eliminated where it already existed in the states

D. the foreign slave trade should be reopened

33. Republican policies toward the South during the post-Civil War Reconstruction Era can be described MOST accurately as   33.___
    A. aiming consistently to protect the interests of post-war big business at the expense of the newly freed slaves
    B. leading to unparalleled corruption among the entrenched carpetbagger governors and their allies in the Black dominated legislatures of the defeated states
    C. leading to significant but only partially implemented constitutional changes on the state level in the South and also on the national level
    D. leading to an effective program of land redistribution that gave to large numbers of newly freed slaves *forty acres and a mule*

34. The strategy of the Confederacy at the start of the Civil War was based on all of the following assumptions EXCEPT: 34.___
    A. Cutting the North in two by seizing Washington and thrusting northward into Maryland and Pennsylvania would force the North to sue for peace
    B. The dependence of Great Britain and France on Southern cotton would lead them to grant diplomatic recognition and give military aid to the Confederacy
    C. Arming the slaves would help the South to offset superior Northern manpower
    D. Southern control of the port of New Orleans would induce the states in the upper Mississippi Valley to join the Confederacy

35. Which one of the following was NOT included in the program advocated by Henry Clay?   35.___
    A. An independent treasury
    B. A protective tariff
    C. Federal aid for internal improvements
    D. A centralized banking system

36. Which one of the following parties reflected a wave of intolerance in the United States?   36.___
    The
    A. Loco-focos   B. Hunkers
    C. Know-Nothings   D. Anti-Masonic Party

37. Which one of the following permitted settlers in the Louisiana Territory to decide the question of slavery for themselves?   37.___
    The
    A. Dred Scott Decision   B. Missouri Compromise
    C. Wilmot Proviso   D. Kansas-Nebraska Act

38. The election of Lincoln to the Presidency in 1860 was   38.___
similar to that of Wilson in 1912 because in each case
the
    A. Democratic candidate won
    B. election had to be decided by the House of Represen-
       tatives
    C. winner benefited by a split in the opposition party
    D. winner scored a huge majority of the popular vote

39. The MAJOR purpose of the blockade during the Civil War   39.___
was to prevent
    A. English volunteers from going to the South
    B. export of cotton to Europe
    C. Confederate officials from going to Europe
    D. the Russian fleet from visiting the South

Question 40.

DIRECTIONS: In Question 40, select the letter preceding the item
           that does NOT belong to the group.

40. Abolitionists   40.___
    A. John Brown   B. William Lloyd Garrison
    C. Abraham Lincoln   D. Harriet Beecher Stowe

41. A section of the United States in which the Democratic   41.___
party had been dominant from 1860 to the 1960's was the
    A. Northeast   B. Middle West
    C. South   D. Far West

42. During most of the 19th century, the United States did   42.___
NOT restrict immigration because
    A. the Bill of Rights forbade restrictions
    B. few Europeans wished to come here
    C. internal expansion created a demand for cheap labor
    D. the rate of population increase was slow

43. *A house divided against itself cannot stand.*   43.___
The author of the above quotation is
    A. Robert E. Lee   B. Daniel Webster
    C. Stephen A. Douglas   D. Abraham Lincoln

44. In the United States, all of the following were important   44.___
concerns of the humanitarians of 1820-30 EXCEPT the
    A. abolition movement
    B. treatment of the insane
    C. public school movement
    D. welfare of migrant laborers

45. All of the following were important cities in the South   45.___
before the Civil War EXCEPT
    A. Atlanta   B. Birmingham
    C. Charleston   D. Richmond

46. The GREATEST opposition in the North to the Compromise of 1850 developed over the
    A. territorial organization of New Mexico and Utah without reference to slavery
    B. assumption of the Texan debt
    C. fugitive slave law
    D. adjustment of the Texan boundary

46.___

47. Which one of the following groups of states seceded AFTER the firing on Fort Sumter?
    A. Maryland, Kentucky, Missouri, Delaware
    B. Texas, Missouri, Virginia, Florida
    C. Virginia, Tennessee, North Carolina, Arkansas
    D. Louisiana, Texas, Virginia, Missouri

47.___

48. Which one of the following was NOT important as a factor in keeping England neutral during the Civil War?
The
    A. sympathy of her commercial class with the Union cause
    B. dependence of England on western wheat
    C. anti-slavery sentiments of English liberals
    D. support of the English working class for the Union cause

48.___

49. Which of the following were characteristic of the economic situation in the United States during the last half of the nineteenth century?
    I. The taking up of free land by farming families
    II. The adoption of a strong national conservation program to preserve our dwindling national resources
  III. The absence of nationwide panics and depressions
    IV. The outbreak of violent strikes, both local and general
    V. Expansion and concentration in industry

The CORRECT answer is:
    A. II, III, IV   B. I, IV, V
    C. I, III, V   D. II, IV, V

49.___

50. When the Missouri Compromise was adopted, which of the following statements about the United States were TRUE?
    I. The Tallmadge amendment to the bill dealing with Missouri's application for statehood had been adopted by both houses of Congress.
    II. Delaware was a slave state.
  III. The *Liberator* had been regularly published for some time.
    IV. The representation of free states in the House of Representatives exceeded the representation of the slave states in the House.

The CORRECT answer is:
    A. I, II   B. II, IV   C. I, III   D. III, IV

50.___

KEY (CORRECT ANSWERS)

1. B	11. B	21. C	31. A	41. C
2. A	12. D	22. C	32. B	42. C
3. C	13. B	23. B	33. C	43. D
4. B	14. C	24. D	34. C	44. D
5. C	15. A	25. D	35. A	45. B
6. D	16. C	26. D	36. C	46. C
7. A	17. C	27. C	37. D	47. C
8. D	18. A	28. C	38. C	48. A
9. B	19. C	29. B	39. B	49. B
10. D	20. D	30. A	40. C	50. B

EXAMINATION SECTION
TEST 1

DIRECTIONS: Each question or incomplete statement is followed by several suggested answers or completions. Select the one that BEST answers the question or completes the statement. *PRINT THE LETTER OF THE CORRECT ANSWER IN THE SPACE AT THE RIGHT.*

1. Most of the iron and munitions used by Confederacy during the war were manufactured in the state of
   A. South Carolina   B. Alabama
   C. Virginia   D. Tennessee

1.___

2. At the outset of the war, the main advantage of the South over the North was a
   A. defensive military posture
   B. long martial tradition
   C. superior navy
   D. larger population pool from which to draw forces

2.___

3. Which of the following Northern states was the last to emancipate its slaves?
   A. Massachusetts   B. New York
   C. Pennsylvania   D. New Jersey

3.___

4. Most of the *carpetbaggers* who came to the South in post-war years were
   A. privateers from New England who sought business opportunity
   B. Union army veterans who had fought in the South
   C. politicians with no base of support in the North
   D. native Southerners who were repatriating

4.___

5. The Crittenden Compromise, proposed in 1860, would have protected slavery in the _____ territory for as long as the area held territorial status.
   I. Utah   II. New Mexico
   III. Kansas   IV. Nebraska

   The CORRECT answer is:
   A. I, II   B. II *only*
   C. I, III, IV   D. III, IV

5.___

6. The South had made considerable progress toward developing its own industrial boom in the 1850s. Which of the following offers the best explanation for why it never grew to play a major role in the Southern economy?
   A. Tariffs and other barriers were repeatedly imposed by the Northern-dominated legislature.
   B. It was impossible, because of slavery, to secure foreign investment in industrial enterprise.

6.___

   C. Most Southerners did not think industry would become
      a significant economic factor.
   D. Most of the capital in the south was invested in
      slave-maintained plantations.

7. For generations after the Civil War, the stronghold of   7.___
   Republican sentiment throughout the Solid South was
   concentrated in the
      A. Mississippi Delta   B. Gulf Coast region
      C. Southern highlands   D. smaller benchlands

8. With his repulse at Sabine Pass in 1863, which Union   8.___
   general was forced to abandon his plan of an amphibious
   invasion of Texas?
      A. George Thomas   B. Nathaniel P. Banks
      C. David Farragut   D. Benjamin Butler

9. The seat of the pro-slavery puppet government that was   9.___
   established in *Bleeding Kansas* was located in
      A. Shawnee Mission   B. Topeka
      C. Wyandotte   D. Wichita

10. Which of the following was the first Indian tribe to   10.___
    declare an allegiance to the Confederate cause in 1861?
       A. Chickasaw B. Miami   C. Cherokee   D. Choctaw

11. Throughout the war effort, northern blacks made several   11.___
    significant contributions toward assisting slaves who had
    been liberated from the South. The most noteworthy of
    these was probably
       A. the provision of medical care for freed slaves and
          their families
       B. the establishment of schools for children of freed
          slaves
       C. political lobbying for the cause of abolition
       D. the organization of freed slaves into self-sufficient
          urban enclaves

12. On February 4, 1861, the new provisional government of the   12.___
    Confederate States of America was organized in
       A. Atlanta   B. Richmond
       C. Columbia   D. Montgomery

13. Which of the following played the largest role in the   13.___
    Union's financing of its war effort?
       A. Taxation
       B. The issuance of *greenback* paper currency
       C. Bond sales
       D. Tariffs

14. At the outset of the war, the strategy that President   14.___
    Lincoln appeared determined to pursue was that of
       A. establishing a border around the Confederacy to assure
          Southerners of goodwill, and wait for Union sentiment
          to overtake the state governments

    B. aggressive penetration and defeat of the South
    C. entering Southern territory for the sole purpose of
       locating and recruiting Southern Unionists
    D. relying solely on a naval blockade to bring economic
       pressure to the South

15. The candidate of the Know-Nothing Party in the election   15.___
    of 1856 was
       A. Martin Van Buren   B. John Fremont
       C. Millard Fillmore   D. Abraham Lincoln

16. For both the North and the South, the most crucial border   16.___
    state throughout the war was
       A. Delaware   B. West Virginia
       C. Tennessee   D. Maryland

17. Which of the following was/were reasons for the failure   17.___
    of the Confederacy's attempts at *Cotton Diplomacy* with
    Britain during the Civil War?
       I. Decreased demand for cotton in Britain
      II. Increased British cotton imports from Egypt and India
     III. A bad grain harvest in Britain, remedied by United
          States grain imports
      IV. Union sales of captured cotton to Britain

    The CORRECT answer is:
       A. I *only*   B. I, III
       C. II, III, IV   D. I, II, III, IV

18. The *black codes* adopted by former Confederate states in   18.___
    1865-1866 generally imposed restrictions on each of the
    following for freed slaves EXCEPT
       A. assembly   B. ownership of land
       C. ownership of weapons   D. travel

19. The Civil Rights Bill which eventually became the 14th   19.___
    Amendment to the Constitution was passed by Congress in
       A. 1864   B. 1866   C. 1870   D. 1874

20. Late in the war, which of the following was a term some-   20.___
    times used as a synonym for a Confederate soldier?
       A. Butternut   B. Grayneck
       C. Roundhead   D. Copperhead

21. The final battle of Gen. George Gordon Meade's Overland   21.___
    Campaign was fought in 1864 at
       A. North Anna   B. Cold Harbor
       C. Spotsylvania   D. Fort Fisher

22. Union forces at the 1864 battle at Nashville were led by   22.___
       A. George Thomas   B. John A. Logan
       C. John M. Schofield   D. George Gordon Meade

23. The *Liberator*, an abolitionary newspaper, was first   23.___
    published in 1831 by
       A. Elijah Lovejoy   B. William Lloyd Garrison
       C. Frederick Douglass   D. John Brown

24. After Lincoln's victory in the 1860 presidential election,   24.___
    Southern Democrats controlled the
       I. House   II. Senate
     III. Supreme Court

    The CORRECT answer is:
       A. I, II   B. III *only*
       C. II *only*   D. I, II, III, IV

25. Who was the first field commander of Union forces in the   25.___
    Civil War?
       A. Irvin McDowell   B. Nathaniel Lyon
       C. Winfield Scott   D. George McClellan

26. Which of the following generals was responsible for over-   26.___
    seeing the reconstruction process in the state of Texas?
       A. Daniel Sickles   B. William Sherman
       C. John Pope   D. Philip Sheridan

27. The main reason for the relatively higher casualty rate   27.___
    among black Union soldiers, compared to whites, was that
       A. they were added to Union regiments late in the war
          without proper training
       B. they were generally ordered into more dangerous combat
          situations
       C. they outnumbered white soldiers in close combat
       D. Confederate officers would kill black soldiers
          rather than take them prisoner

28. From the beginning of his administration, Andrew Johnson   28.___
    suffered from a number of serious disadvantages. Which
    of the following was NOT one of these?
       A. Public rumors of drunkenness and misconduct
       B. Stubbornness and inflexibility
       C. A fundamental lack of integrity
       D. The nature of the political support attracted by
          his reconstruction plan

29. The second state to secede from the Union, on January 9,   29.___
    1861, was
       A. Georgia   B. Mississippi
       C. Louisiana   D. Florida

30. The primary concern of most Americans immediately follow-   30.___
    ing the war was
       A. recovering from a post-war economic slump
       B. the problem of restoring the former Confederate states
       C. the mode of punishment for those who had rebelled
       D. the status of the institution of slavery in the South

31. The *Bloody Angle* was an area of heavy fighting in the   31.___
    battle at
    A. Gettysburg   B. Antietam
    C. Spotsylvania   D. Shiloh

32. The first important policy battle between President Lincoln 32.___
    and congressional Radical Republicans was fought over the
    readmission of _____ to the Union.
    A. Arkansas   B. South Carolina
    C. Louisiana   D. Tennessee

33. Approximately what percentage of Southern whites were   33.___
    slave owners in the antebellum South?
    A. 25   B. 45   C. 65   D. 85

34. The party responsible for the failure of the 1860 Critten- 34.___
    den Compromise was
    A. the Supreme Court
    B. the House of Representatives
    C. Abraham Lincoln
    D. the Senate

35. The Confederate Department of Alabama and West Florida,   35.___
    whose primary wartime responsibilities were defending
    Mobile and Pensacola from naval attack, was commanded by
    A. Maj. Gen. Stephen D. Lee
    B. Maj. Gen. Braxton Bragg
    C. Joseph E. Johnston
    D. Lt. Gen. Leonidas Polk

36. At the outset of 1863, the only military operations that   36.___
    would have a bearing upon the outcome of the war were
    those in
    A. Virginia and the Carolinas
    B. Virginia and Kentucky
    C. the Carolinas and Georgia
    D. Texas and Virginia

37. Each of the following was an element of the 1860 compromise 37.___
    advocated by Kentucky Senator John Crittenden EXCEPT
    A. the prohibition of slavery above the Missouri Com-
       promise line
    B. compensation to owners of *rescued* slaves
    C. emancipation in the District of Columbia
    D. the self-determination of future new states regarding
       slavery

38. By far, the most active state in the operation of the   38.___
    underground railroad was
    A. Ohio   B. Illinois
    C. Pennsylvania   D. Iowa

39. In the antebellum South, where slaves were often given   39.___
    religious instruction, these teachings most often empha-
    sized
        A. ritual   B. faith   C. doctrine   D. morality

40. Each of the following was a *political* general in the Union 40.___
    Army EXCEPT
        A. Daniel Sickles   B. James Garfield
        C. Irvin McDowell   D. Benjamin Butler

41. Which of the following cities served as the starting point   41.___
    for General Sherman's march to the sea?
        A. Atlanta   B. Bowling Green
        C. Chattanooga   D. Knoxville

42. Which of the following was NOT an element of the *Anaconda* 42.___
    Plan proposed by Union General-in-Chief Winfield Scott in
    1861?
    A
        A. march from the Mississippi River to the Atlantic
        B. strong line of Federal positions on the Western border
        C. strong thrust down the Mississippi Valley
        D. blockade of Southern ports

43. Approximately what percentage of the Union's armed forces   43.___
    were composed of foreign-born men?
        A. 5   B. 10   C. 20   D. 40

44. In which Southern state was Jefferson Davis captured by   44.___
    Union forces in April of 1865?
        A. Georgia   B. South Carolina
        C. Florida   D. Virginia

45. In the eyes of many observers, the 1864 Battle of Cold   45.___
    Harbor proved that
        A. Union troops were much more poorly trained and disci-
           plined than their Confederate counterparts
        B. cavalry alone could not win a battle
        C. the Confederates were unwilling to negotiate any terms
           other than total independence
        D. the Union was willing to sacrifice a high number of
           casualties to ensure victory

46. Which of the following served as the Confederate secretary   46.___
    of the navy?
        A. George W. Randolph   B. John C. Breckinridge
        C. Leroy Pope Walker   D. Stephen Mallory

47. Each of the following was considered to be a stronghold   47.___
    of *Copperheads* in the North during the latter years of the
    war EXCEPT
        A. Illinois   B. Michigan
        C. Indiana   D. Ohio

48. Which of the following states attempted to remain neutral   48.___
    in the Civil War after its secession delegates refused
    to secede?
       A. Kentucky   B. Missouri   C. Maryland   D. Delaware

49. Regarding the readmission of the Southern states to the   49.___
    Union, President Lincoln's belief seems to have been that
       A. the establishment of a representative government,
          with a proportionate number of black legislators,
          would be sufficient
       B. they had forfeited all their rights and must undergo
          the same process as any other territory for acceptance
          as a state
       C. it would be up to Congress to devise the conditions
          under which readmission would be carried out
       D. since they had never legally withdrawn, it would be a
          simple and informal matter

50. Among the following religious groups, which played the   50.___
    most important role in antebellum abolitionist leadership?
       A. Unitarians   B. Methodists
       C. Episcopalians   D. Roman Catholics

———

KEY (CORRECT ANSWERS)

1. B	11. B	21. B	31. C	41. C
2. A	12. D	22. A	32. A	42. A
3. D	13. C	23. B	33. A	43. C
4. B	14. B	24. D	34. C	44. A
5. B	15. C	25. A	35. B	45. D
6. D	16. D	26. D	36. A	46. D
7. C	17. D	27. D	37. C	47. B
8. B	18. B	28. C	38. A	48. B
9. A	19. B	29. B	39. D	49. D
10. D	20. A	30. A	40. C	50. B

TEST 2

DIRECTIONS: Each question or incomplete statement is followed by several suggested answers or completions. Select the one that BEST answers the question or completes the statement. *PRINT THE LETTER OF THE CORRECT ANSWER IN THE SPACE AT THE RIGHT.*

1. During the war, much of the outrage felt by Southerners concerning their treatment at the hands of Union forces centered on the example of General Benjamin Butler's occupation of the city of
   A. Pensacola
   B. Jackson
   C. New Orleans
   D. Mobile

   1.___

2. In 1855, abolitionist John Brown and his sons traveled to _____ to make it a haven for antislavery settlers.
   A. Oregon Territory
   B. West Virginia
   C. New Mexico Territory
   D. Kansas

   2.___

3. Economic growth in the North during the war was fueled by each of the following factors EXCEPT
   A. the invention and mass production of the mechanical reaper
   B. the expansion of the labor market by the addition of freed slaves
   C. protective tariffs
   D. profiteering

   3.___

4. During the first forty years after the American Revolution, Southerners were often divided among themselves on political issues. Among these, the most divisive was probably
   A. civil rights
   B. international trade
   C. banking and financial policy
   D. slavery and abolitionism

   4.___

5. Which of the following is generally considered to be U.S. Grant's best-fought campaign of the Civil War?
   A. Vicksburg
   B. Lookout Mountain
   C. Port Hudson
   D. Shiloh

   5.___

6. From 1863 onward, which Southern state was divided into two civil government jurisdictions, one Unionist and one Confederate?
   A. Louisiana
   B. Tennessee
   C. Arkansas
   D. North Carolina

   6.___

7. After the congressional elections of 1866, the first action undertaken by the Radical Republican Congress was to
   A. impose military reconstruction on the Southern states
   B. exclude the Southern votes from the electoral college

   7.___

     C. refute the legitimacy of the existing state governments
        in the former Confederate states
     D. bar Southern representatives from the House and Senate
        indefinitely

8. Throughout most of the war, the primary mission of the   8.___
Army of the Potomac was to
     A. inflict irreversible damage and loss upon the Army of
        Northern Virginia
     B. defend Washington
     C. protect Chesapeake ports from land assaults
     D. capture Richmond

9. The main reason for Lincoln's replacement of George Gordon   9.___
Meade with U.S. Grant as commander of the Army of the
Potomac was that
     A. Grant had powerful allies in the Lincoln cabinet
     B. Meade had not aggressively pursued General Lee's army
        after the victory at Gettysburg
     C. Grant's Western campaigns had been more successful
        than any Union campaign to date
     D. Meade had not protected his flank at Gettysburg and
        nearly lost the battle

10. The first important reconstruction act, passed in 1867, was 10.___
largely the work of
     A. Thaddeus Stevens   B. Andrew Johnson
     C. Charles Sumner   D. John Sherman

11. The primary idea behind the Declaration of Immediate   11.___
Causes, drafted by Christopher Memminger in 1860, was that
     A. blacks and whites were considered unequal under the
        terms of the United States Constitution
     B. Lincoln's suspension of the writ of habeas corpus
        was illegal
     C. the attack on Fort Sumter was an act of defense
     D. South Carolina was justified in seceding from the
        Union

12. In what way did the Republicans avert defeat in the   12.___
election of 1864?
     A. Placing Andrew Johnson on the ticket
     B. Tabling the issue of emancipation
     C. *Supervision* of balloting in the border states
     D. Joining with War Democrats to form the Union Party

13. In both the Union and Confederate armed forces, the *buck* 13.___
and gag was a
     A. means of hauling a battery and ordnance
     B. strategy for striking the flank of an opponent
     C. means of punishing enlisted men
     D. type of musket load

14. The last state to secede from the Union in June of 1861   14.___
    was
       A. Texas   B. Virginia   C. Arkansas   D. Tennessee

15. Lincoln's Emancipation Proclamation formally freed slaves   15.___
    in
         I. specific conquered areas in the South
        II. the Confederate states still in rebellion
       III. the border states
        IV. all United States territories

    The CORRECT answer is:
       A. I, II   B. II *only*
       C. II, III, IV   D. III, IV

16. Which of the following served as secretary of the navy in   16.___
    the administration of Abraham Lincoln?
       A. Gideon Welles   B. Edward Bates
       C. David Farragut   D. Simon Cameron

17. Which of the following statements about the American   17.___
    Colonization Society is true?
       A. Its chapters existed mostly in northern states.
       B. Most of its funds were directed toward establishing
          a colony of free blacks in Africa.
       C. It was more extreme than most abolitionist groups.
       D. It was initially dominated by northern abolitionists.

18. In the mid-1800s, the statehood of _____ appears to be the   18.___
    event that permanently tipped the balance of sectional
    power to the North.
       A. Oregon   B. California C. Colorado D. Kansas

19. The outbreak of the Civil War sparked a renewed debate in   19.___
    the North about the nature of black Americans. Most of
    the abolitionists based their arguments for racial equality
    on
       A. physical and mental capacities
       B. the Christian doctrine that all were equal in the
          sight of God
       C. cultural differences
       D. the words of the United States Constitution

20. The most populous state of the deep South was   20.___
       A. Florida   B. Mississippi
       C. Alabama   D. Georgia

21. Which of the following offers the best explanation for   21.___
    the Republicans' selection of Andrew Johnson as Lincoln's
    running mate in the 1864 election?
    He was
       A. a former slaveowner who could attract votes from the
          border states
       B. an intellectual who could strike a balance to Lincoln's
          folksy, unread image

    C. a staunch Lincoln loyalist who would galvanize the
       electorate
    D. little-known and therefore inoffensive to voters

22. Which of the following was a heavy artillery piece,   22.___
    invented by the Confederates, that saw service both on
    ironclads and in seacoast fortifications?
    A. Blakely gun   B. Dahlgren gun
    C. Brooke rifle   D. Howitzer

23. The Confederate victory that gave General Lee the confi-   23.___
    dence to launch a second invasion of the north occurred
    in 1863 at
    A. Petersburg   B. Spotsylvania
    C. Chancellorsville   D. Antietam

24. Which of the following factors played the most signifi-   24.___
    cant role in bringing about the Panic of 1857?
    The
    A. Missouri Compromise
    B. collapse of the shipping industry
    C. revocation of the National Bank's charter
    D. overbuilding of railroads

25. General Grant was made general-in-chief of the armed   25.___
    forces after the
    A. battle at Vicksburg
    B. fall of Atlanta
    C. victory at Forts Henry and Donelson
    D. conquest of Chattanooga

26. During the wave of foreign settlement that occurred in   26.___
    the United States in the 1840s and 1850s, which of the
    following states was most strongly *nativist*, or resistant
    to immigrant participation in civil society?
    A. Massachusetts   B. Kentucky
    C. Florida   D. Wisconsin

27. The purpose of the Edmunds Resolution of July 20, 1868   27.___
    was to
    A. take control of the scheduling of congressional
       sessions
    B. assume partial control of the armed forces by gaining
       consensual powers over the army's general-in-chief
    C. give Congress, and not the states, the power to rati-
       fy constitutional amendments
    D. exclude certain Confederate states from the electoral
       college

28. In large part, the Confederacy's war effort was financed   28.___
    by a $500,000 loan from the state of
    A. South Carolina   B. Alabama
    C. Georgia   D. Mississippi

29. Which of the following can fairly be said to be a result   29.____
    of the extreme, violent fringe of the abolitionist move-
    ment in the North?
    The
        I. endangerment of civil rights such as free speech and
           freedom of the press
       II. hastening of the emancipation of United States slaves
           by several years
      III. growth of divisive sectionalism
       IV. deferral of other reform movements

    The CORRECT answer is:
        A. I, III   B. II *only*
        C. I, III, IV   D. I, II, III, IV

30. In which of the following Northern states was slavery   30.____
    prohibited by the Ordinance of 1787?
        A. New Jersey   B. New York
        C. Pennsylvania   D. Ohio

31. The largest cavalry engagement of the Civil War occurred   31.____
    at the Battle of
        A. Brawner's Farm   B. Franklin's Crossing
        C. Horseshoe Ridge   D. Brandy Station

32. The results of the Emancipation Proclamation included   32.____
        I. a splintering of the Southern alliance
       II. an increase in desertion from Union forces
      III. a strengthening of the North's moral cause
       IV. increased opposition to intervention among foreign
           commoners

    The CORRECT answer is:
        A. I, III   B. II, III, IV
        C. III, IV   D. I, II, III, IV

33. The first serious bloodshed of the Civil War occurred   33.____
    just after the inauguration of Abraham Lincoln in riots
    in the streets of
        A. Pittsburgh   B. Alexandria
        C. Baltimore   D. Gettysburg

34. Each of the following Southern states began its recon-   34.____
    struction process under the Lincoln administration EXCEPT
        A. Texas   B. Louisiana
        C. Virginia   D. Tennessee

35. What was the means by which the Confederate states   35.____
    attempted to attract the sympathies of England and France
    during the Civil War?
        A. Offering lucrative shipbuilding contracts
        B. Seeking an endorsement of states' rights
        C. Distributing propaganda about Northern aggression
        D. Withholding cotton exports

36. Of the following Southern states, which was the last to   36.___
    be returned to *home rule* after the process of reconstruc-
    tion?
      A. Florida   B. Alabama   C. Texas   D. Virginia

37. In March of 1865, Confederate General Joseph E. Johnston   37.___
    surrendered to William T. Sherman after losing the battle
    at _____, North Carolina.
      A. Bentonville   B. Averasborough
      C. Fayetteville   D. Goldsboro

38. The Congressional Committee on the Conduct of the War, an   38.___
    entity within the United States Congress during the Civil
    War, could best be described as a
      A. strong moral prosecutor of military misconduct
      B. radical think tank devoted to the cause of emancipa-
         tion
      C. political tool of anti-Lincoln Republicans
      D. fiscally immoderate financer of the Union war effort

39. Which of the following amendments to the Constitution   39.___
    gave the United States Supreme Court the power to protect
    the basic civil rights of all citizens?
      A. Twelfth   B. Thirteenth
      C. Fourteenth   D. Fifteenth

40. Who led the failed Camden expedition in Arkansas in 1864?   40.___
      A. John M. Thayer   B. Nathaniel P. Banks
      C. Thomas Ransom   D. Frederick Steele

41. The most critical foreign crisis facing the United States   41.___
    immediately after the war had to do with a violation of
    the Monroe Doctrine by
      A. Canada   B. Russia   C. France   D. Britain

42. The primary purpose of Blazer's Scouts, a Union force   42.___
    organized by General George Crook, was to
      A. locate and destroy Quantrill and his raiders
      B. hunt down and destroy blockade runners
      C. devalue the Confederate currency through counterfeit-
         ing
      D. destroy the Partisan Rangers operating in Virginia

43. The basic premise of Congress's first reconstruction act,   43.___
    passed in 1867, was that
      A. the Confederacy was an enemy country to be occupied
         by the conquering army
      B. the former Confederate states had never lawfully
         seceded
      C. the former Confederate states, with their large black
         populations, were not practicing representative
         government
      D. no lawful government existed in the seceded states

44. In which of the following states in 1860 did slaves out-   44.___
    number free whites?
    A. Alabama   B. Mississippi
    C. Georgia   D. Louisiana

45. Which of the following was granted statehood in 1861?   45.___
    A. Oregon   B. Colorado
    C. California   D. Kansas

46. Who led the Union Army of the Cumberland at the battle   46.___
    of Chickamauga in September of 1863?
    A. Gordon Granger   B. William S. Rosecrans
    C. Henry Halleck   D. George Armstrong Custer

47. The most significant result of the Supreme Court's 1857   47.___
    Dred Scott decision was that
    A. slavery could not be barred from any United States
       territories
    B. black slaves could not sue in federal courts
    C. the Missouri Compromise was invalidated
    D. black slaves were not considered United States citi-
       zens

48. Shortly after the Virginia Convention approved secession,   48.___
    a small force of Confederate volunteers occupied the city
    of
    A. Alexandria   B. Yorktown
    C. Annapolis   D. Washington, D.C.

49. It was Senator Charles Sumner's scathing oration against   49.___
    the _____ that provoked his beating at the hands of
    Congressman Preston Brooks of South Carolina.
    A. doctrine of nullification
    B. actions of pro-slavery men in Kansas
    C. passage of the Fugitive Slave Law
    D. passage of the Kansas-Nebraska Act

50. Which of the following Confederate states approved   50.___
    secession by the narrowest margin?
    A. Florida   B. Missouri   C. Virginia   D. Arkansas

KEY (CORRECT ANSWERS)

1. C	11. D	21. A	31. D	41. C
2. D	12. D	22. C	32. B	42. D
3. B	13. C	23. C	33. C	43. D
4. C	14. D	24. D	34. A	44. B
5. A	15. B	25. D	35. D	45. D
6. C	16. A	26. B	36. A	46. B
7. D	17. B	27. D	37. A	47. A
8. D	18. B	28. B	38. C	48. A
9. B	19. B	29. D	39. C	49. B
10. D	20. D	30. D	40. D	50. C

TEST 3

DIRECTIONS: Each question or incomplete statement is followed by several suggested answers or completions. Select the one that BEST answers the question or completes the statement. *PRINT THE LETTER OF THE CORRECT ANSWER IN THE SPACE AT THE RIGHT.*

1. Which of the following was an anti-slavery activist who died defending his press in Alton, Illinois in 1837?
   A. Charles Francis Adams
   B. William Wells Brown
   C. William Lloyd Garrison
   D. Elijah Lovejoy

   1.___

2. In which of the following states were slaves freed by the 13th Amendment, rather than by state legislation or the Emancipation Proclamation?
   A. West Virginia
   B. Arkansas
   C. Kentucky
   D. Tennessee

   2.___

3. On February 17, 1865,
   A. the Union Department of California was folded into the Department of the Pacific
   B. the city of Charleston was evacuated in anticipation of the arrival of Gen. William Sherman
   C. the first Confederate blockade runner was captured by the U.S.S. Sabine of the Union Navy
   D. Thomas *Stonewall* Jackson died of pneumonia

   3.___

4. After the Battle of Antietam, President Lincoln replaced Gen. George McClellan with
   A. George Thomas
   B. Joseph Hooker
   C. Henry Halleck
   D. Ambrose E. Burnside

   4.___

5. Throughout the Civil War, compared to their eastern counterparts, Union soldiers from the West were generally most different in their
   A. ratio of losses to victories
   B. questionable loyalty
   C. average age
   D. lack of discipline

   5.___

6. In the 1861 Battle of Bird Creek, Confederate Colonel Douglas Cooper led about 1,400 soldiers against a group of about 1,000 pro-Union Indians composed mostly of
   A. Choctaws and Chickasaws
   B. Cherokees and Creeks
   C. Seminoles and Cherokees
   D. Creeks and Seminoles

   6.___

7. The results of the 1858 Lincoln-Douglas debates included
   I. Lincoln's defeat of Douglas for the Senate seat
   II. the alienation of Southern Democrats from Douglas
   III. the rise of Lincoln to national prominence

   7.___

The CORRECT answer is:
  A. I *only*   B. I, II   C. II, III   D. III *only*

8. Which of the following states did Abraham Lincoln win in   8.___
    the election of 1864?
      A. New Jersey   B. Kentucky
      C. Maryland   D. Delaware

9. On December 20, 1860, the *Committee of Thirteen* met in   9.___
      A. Richmond to draft the new Confederate Constitution
      B. Washington to plan the offensive strategy of the
         Union Army
      C. Montgomery to vote on secession
      D. Washington to attempt to avert disunion

10. In what year were all Confederate war leaders granted a   10.___
    presidential pardon?
      A. 1866   B. 1868   C. 1870   D. 1877

11. Which of the following states was most generally opposed   11.___
    to the idea of secession?
      A. Maryland   B. Kentucky   C. Delaware   D. Missouri

12. The _____ probably did the most to drive the nation to   12.___
    Civil War.
      A. Fugitive Slave Act of 1853
      B. Kansas-Nebraska Act
      C. Compromise of 1850
      D. Wilmot Proviso

13. Ideally, a Civil War field battery consisted of _____ guns   13.___
    of the same caliber.
      A. 2   B. 4   C. 6   D. 8

14. Which of the following cities served as the Union point   14.___
    of departure for nearly all Union efforts to open the
    upper Mississippi or penetrate into the Southern interior?
      A. Cairo   B. St. Louis
      C. Bowling Green   D. Louisville

15. Which of the following was the presidential candidate of   15.___
    the Free Soil Party in the 1848 elections?
      A. Frederick Douglass   B. Martin Van Buren
      C. William Lloyd Garrison D. John Brown

16. Which of the following Southern states was readmitted to   16.___
    the Union on June 25, 1868, but returned to military
    control after expelling blacks from its legislature?
      A. Virginia   B. Georgia   C. Arkansas   D. Texas

17. Among the reasons for the basic instability of the Con-   17.___
    federate government, the most significant was probably
      A. the effectiveness of Union intrigue
      B. the youth and inexperience of its membership

    C. the disagreement over the location of the capital city
    D. its predication on the right to secession

18. Historians generally agree that the most important factor   18.___
    in the downfall of the Confederacy was the
    A. destruction of the Southern countryside
    B. Union naval blockade of Southern ports
    C. spread of popular abolitionist sentiment
    D. force of the Union armies

19. The first fighting to occur between elements of the North   19.___
    and South after Lincoln's inauguration took place in
    A. Texas   B. New York
    C. Florida   D. South Carolina

20. In part, the Confederacy's war effort was financed by a   20.___
    loan from the treasury of
    A. Germany   B. France
    C. the Netherlands   D. Great Britain

21. The battle at _____ in 1865 is generally thought to be   21.___
    the last battle of any importance in the Civil War.
    A. Goldsboro   B. Lynchburg
    C. Petersburg   D. Five Forks

22. The purpose of the Force Acts, passed by Congress in 1870   22.___
    and 1871, was to
    A. permit military enforcement of black suffrage in the
       South
    B. permit military supervision of state legislatures in
       the South
    C. invalidate the *black codes* adopted by several states
    D. protect blacks from the violence of night-riding
       terrorists

23. The fourth state to leave the Union on January 11, 1861 was 23.___
    A. Alabama   B. Tennessee
    C. Kentucky   D. Georgia

24. Which of Andrew Johnson's cabinet members was secretly   24.___
    serving congressional radical Republicans as a spy and
    informer?
    A. W. W. Holden   B. Carl Schurz
    C. Edwin M. Stanton   D. Henry Stanbery

25. During the mid-1800s, the people of the South increasingly   25.___
    turned from a strong nationalist tendency toward section-
    alism. Which of the following was NOT an important factor
    that helped to bring about this shift?
    A. Reaction to legislation that seemed designed to help
       the North while inhibiting the South
    B. A long agricultural depression that ended in 1832
    C. The perception that slavery was a doomed institution
    D. The invention of the cotton gin

26. The first Civil War engagement between Generals Grant and   26.___
    Lee took place at
    A. Spotsylvania   B. Manassas Junction
    C. Cold Harbor   D. Plank Road

27. The *Bread Riot* of 1863 occurred in the Confederate city of 27.___
    A. Montgomery   B. Savannah
    C. Richmond   D. Augusta

28. The most significant reason for Stephen Douglas's loss   28.___
    of the 1960 presidential election to Abraham Lincoln was
    that
    A. Lincoln was able to win a small measure of support
       in the South
    B. Lincoln carried the most populous states
    C. the new states of California and Oregon made the
       difference
    D. Southern Democrats had split from Douglas's party to
       nominate another candidate

29. The Union Army that was formed latest in the war was the   29.___
    Army of
    A. the Southwest   B. the Shenandoah
    C. Kansas   D. the Frontier

30. In the Confederate national campaign of 1863, Jefferson   30.___
    Davis was criticized by opponents for his policies con-
    cerning each of the following EXCEPT
    A. taxation   B. habeas corpus
    C. property rights   D. conscription

31. Which of the following industries did NOT experience   31.___
    wartime growth in the North?
    A. Agriculture   B. Textiles
    C. Petroleum   D. Maritime shipping

32. A Union defeat at the battle of Shiloh was prevented by   32.___
    the arrival, on the evening of the first day, of the
    army of General
    A. U.S. Grant   B. Philip Sheridan
    C. Don Carlos Buell   D. William T. Sherman

33. Of the following, which was the last Southern city to   33.___
    fall under Union control in the latter years of the war?
    A. Wilmington   B. Richmond
    C. Montgomery   D. Mobile

34. In 1860, the U.S. Navy Yard at Norfolk was captured by   34.___
    Confederate forces, largely because the Union had failed
    to send military reinforcements. Which of the following
    best explains the Union's failure to protect the installa-
    tion?
    A. The inability to stem Confederate traffic through the
       city of Baltimore
    B. A lack of anticipation by the secretary of the navy

C. A preoccupation with the blockade of Southern ports
D. A reluctance to alienate the people of a state that had not yet declared secession

35. According to the beliefs of Andrew Johnson, which of the following had been Union goals for the prosecution of the Civil War?
    I. Preservation of the Union
    II. Emancipation
    III. The equal status of whites and free blacks

    The CORRECT answer is:
    A. I *only*   B. I, II   C. II *only*   D. III *only*

35.___

36. During the early 1800s, even many Northerners were inhospitable to free blacks. In particular, immigrants from _____ were hostile to blacks, whom they viewed as wage-lowerers.
    A. Mexico   B. Poland   C. Ireland   D. Germany

36.___

37. In what year was the importation of slaves to the United States made illegal?
    A. 1787   B. 1808   C. 1848   D. 1865

37.___

38. Which of the following military commanders was NOT involved in the battle of Antietam?
    A. Ulysses S. Grant
    B. Robert E. Lee
    C. Thomas J. *Stonewall* Jackson
    D. George McClellan

38.___

39. The legacies of the reconstruction era of the United States generally include each of the following EXCEPT the
    A. emergence of the Federal government's precedence over states' rights
    B. rejection of complaints against majoritarianism in American government
    C. dominance of industrial over agrarian economic forces
    D. rejection of caste as the basis for the American social order

39.___

40. Which of the following cities was known to have strong Southern sympathies throughout the Civil War?
    A. New York   B. Boston
    C. Philadelphia   D. Chicago

40.___

41. Following an initial post-war slump, the economy in the North underwent a remarkable resurgence, which was most evident in the field of
    A. petroleum refining   B. railroad building
    C. home construction   D. steel processing

41.___

42. Which of the following factors best explains the cautious   42.___
    nature of President Lincoln's first military measures of
    the war?
    A. Inexperience in military matters
    B. The fear of suffering a major loss that could terminate
       the Northern numerical advantage
    C. The fear of sparking foreign interest in the cause of
       the South
    D. The fear of alienating border states

43. Which of the following Southern states seceded from the   43.___
    Union after the incident at Fort Sumter?
    A. Louisiana   B. Georgia
    C. Texas   D. North Carolina

44. Who was responsible for the 1863 sacking of Lawrence,   44.___
    Kansas and the later Massacre at Baxter Springs?
    A. James Blunt   B. Frank James
    C. John Robert Baylor   D. William Quantrill

45. The Republican Party in the United States was formed by   45.___
    a politically varied collection of people who were general-
    ly united in reaction against the
    A. Kansas-Nebraska Act   B. Fugitive Slave Act
    C. writ of habeas corpus D. Gadsden Purchase

46. Most of the Quaker-operated *underground railroad stations*   46.___
    were located in the state of
    A. Iowa   B. Indiana
    C. Illinois   D. Tennessee

47. Abraham Lincoln's Democratic opponent in the election of   47.___
    1864 was
    A. Clement Vallandigham   B. Benjamin Wade
    C. George McClellan   D. Salmon P. Chase

48. The common tactical infantry and cavalry unit of the   48.___
    Civil War was the
    A. company   B. brigade   C. regiment   D. corps

49. During his conduct of the Union war effort, Abraham   49.___
    Lincoln committed several violations of the United States
    Constitution, including
      I. suspension of the writ of habeas corpus
     II. military supervision of elections
    III. direct appropriation of advance funding from the
         Treasury for military purposes
     IV. increasing the size of the United States army without
         congressional approval

    The CORRECT answer is:
    A. I *only*   B. I, III, IV
    C. I, III   D. I, II, III, IV

50. What was the term used to denote civilians who were   50.___
    officially appointed to supply soldiers with a list of
    approved items such as food, cutlery, newspapers, and
    books?
        A. Contrabands   B. Factors
        C. Vivandieres   D. Sutlers

—

KEY (CORRECT ANSWERS)

1. D	11. C	21. D	31. D	41. B
2. C	12. B	22. D	32. C	42. D
3. B	13. C	23. A	33. C	43. D
4. D	14. A	24. C	34. D	44. D
5. D	15. B	25. C	35. B	45. A
6. D	16. B	26. D	36. C	46. A
7. C	17. D	27. C	37. B	47. C
8. C	18. B	28. B	38. A	48. B
9. D	19. C	29. B	39. B	49. D
10. B	20. B	30. C	40. A	50. D

—

TEST 4

DIRECTIONS: Each question or incomplete statement is followed by
               several suggested answers or completions. Select the
               one that BEST answers the question or completes the
               statement. *PRINT THE LETTER OF THE CORRECT ANSWER IN
               THE SPACE AT THE RIGHT.*

1. The first list of accusations against President Johnson   1.___
    that were *investigated* by Congress in 1867 -- a prelude
    to the coming impeachment process -- included each of the
    following EXCEPT
        A. violation of the Tenure-of-Office Act
        B. corrupt use of veto and appointing powers
        C. complicity in the Lincoln assassination
        D. the pardon of Confederate officials and military
           personnel

2. Who was the Union Army's chief of staff at the outset of   2.___
    the Civil War?
        A. George McClellan   B. Winfield Scott
        C. Benjamin Butler   D. Irvin McDowell

3. The stance of most antebellum *free-soilers* was that   3.___
        A. slavery should be abolished outright in the South
        B. slavery should be gradually phased out by individual
           Southern state legislatures
        C. the institution should not be abolished but should be
           prohibited in the territories
        D. nobody born within the United States should be a slave
           under any circumstances

4. The first battle of Bull Run was fought along a Confederate   4.___
    line of defense known as the
        A. Tar Meridian   B. Skein
        C. Alexandria Line   D. Lookout Ridge

5. In 1877, federal troops were finally withdrawn from the   5.___
    states of _____, as a result of the Hayes-Tilden electoral
    bargain.
        A. Louisiana and South Carolina
        B. Mississippi and Alabama
        C. North Carolina and South Carolina
        D. Florida and Georgia

6. Which of the following was a slave state throughout the   6.___
    Civil War?
        A. Missouri   B. Maryland
        C. West Virginia   D. Delaware

7. A(n) _____ can be said to have considerably prolonged the   7.___
    war for the North.
       A. over-reliance on naval superiority
       B. preoccupation with defeating General Lee and the Army
          of Northern Virginia
       C. underestimation of the Southern resolve
       D. failure to develop a coherent strategy on the Western
          front

8. Who commanded the Confederate Army of Tennessee in 1864?   8._____
       A. James Longstreet
       B. Braxton Bragg
       C. Thomas J. *Stonewall* Jackson
       D. Joseph E. Johnston

9. After the war had ended, how many Confederates, excluding   9.___
    the Lincoln assassination conspirators, were eventually
    executed for the commission of war crimes?
       A. 0   B. 1   C. 7   D. 13

10. Throughout the war, the Confederate cabinet was served by   10.___
    at least one man from each of the following states EXCEPT
       A. South Carolina   B. Tennessee
       C. Kentucky   D. North Carolina

11. The general plan of Northern attack during the Civil War   11.___
    evolved to include four main elements. Which of the
    following was NOT one of these?
       A. Strangulation through the capture of Richmond
       B. Suffocation through blockade
       C. Bisection through control of the Mississippi River
       D. Penetration through control of the Shenandoah Valley

12. The Confederacy's gap in war matériel was closed in large   12.___
    part by the prodigious output of the powder works of
    George W. Rains at
       A. Raleigh, North Carolina B. Montgomery, Alabama
       C. Lynchburg, Virginia   D. Augusta, Georgia

13. Who was the Whig candidate for president in the election   13.___
    of 1852?
       A. Daniel Webster   B. Abraham Lincoln
       C. Franklin Pierce   D. Winfield Scott

14. By 1863, it was estimated by the United States (Union)   14.___
    government that the Civil War was costing about _____ daily.
       A. $750,000   B. $1.2 million
       C. $2.5 million   D. $4.6 million

15. While George McClellan was assuming command of the Army of   15.___
    the Potomac, Union forces suffered a defeat at _____, which
    resulted in the loss of General Nathaniel Lyon and the
    demotion of General John C. Fremont.
       A. Balls Bluff, Virginia B. Corinth, Mississippi
       C. Cairo, Illinois   D. Wilson's Creek, Missouri

16. Each of the following was a trend in Southern life in the   16.___
    decades before the outbreak of war EXCEPT
    A. poor farmers accepted the status quo
    B. trained urban professionals switched to agriculture
       for reasons of social status
    C. the overall value of land decreased slightly
    D. the number of poor whites increased at a greater rate
       than that of slaveholding whites

17. At war's end, the most serious problems for the South   17.___
    were _____ in nature.
    A. economic   B. political
    C. social   D. psychological

18. The first Southern port to be blockaded by the north was   18.___
    _____, in 1861.
    A. Pensacola   B. Charleston
    C. New Orleans   D. Wilmington

19. The Southern cause of secession received open sympathy   19.___
    from the ruling classes of each of the following foreign
    countries EXCEPT
    A. France   B. Russia
    C. Germany   D. Great Britain

20. What was the term (in both the North and the South) for a   20.___
    unit of 50-100 soldiers commanded by a captain?
    A. Regiment   B. Company   C. Platoon   D. Brigade

21. The main idea of the fateful *Freeport Doctrine* expressed   21.___
    by Stephen Douglas during his debates with Abraham Lincoln
    was that
    A. the Supreme Court's Dred Scott decision was rightfully
       the law of the land
    B. territories should be allowed self-determination on
       the issue of slavery
    C. the sectional balance among states and territories
       should be preserved at all costs
    D. the Missouri Compromise never should have been invali-
       dated

22. In the conflict known as *Bleeding Kansas*, who carried out 22.___
    the so-called 1856 Potawatomi Massacre?
    A. Dave Poole   B. William Quantrill
    C. Frank James   D. John Brown

23. When Northern lawmakers criticized the 1853 Gadsden   23.___
    Purchase of an area of land from Mexico, their complaints
    centered on the
    A. cost of the purchase in light of its apparent useful-
       ness
    B. practice of slavery that was rumored to be in opera-
       tion in the territory
    C. possibility of a land grab by Southern sectionalists
    D. circumvention of Senate approval

24. At the outbreak of the war, the leading abolitionist in   24.___
    the United States House of Representatives was
    A. Charles Francis Adams   B. Thaddeus Stevens
    C. Sidney George Fisher   D. Charles Sumner

25. The *Middle Phase* of the Civil War included each of the   25.___
    following battles EXCEPT
    A. Chattanooga   B. Atlanta
    C. Vicksburg   D. Gettysburg

26. The first anti-slavery political organization in the   26.___
    United States was the _____ Party, organized in 1840.
    A. Free Soil   B. Free Chattel
    C. Liberty   D. Know-Nothing

27. Which of the following newspapers was the leading anti-   27.___
    administration advocate of slavery and secession in the
    Southern United States?
    The
    A. Columbia *South Carolinian*
    B. Charleston *Mercury*
    C. Baltimore *Sun*
    D. Kansas City *Star*

28. Probably the most important rendezvous point for   28.___
    Confederate blockade-runners throughout the Civil War was
    A. Havana   B. Halifax
    C. Cape Hatteras   D. Nassau

29. For what reason did foreign governments sympathetic to   29.___
    the Confederacy not attempt to break through the Northern
    blockade during the war?
    A. They did not want to risk a war with the Union.
    B. They thought it would constitute a violation of the
       Monroe Doctrine.
    C. They had an adequate corps of privateers to do the
       job for them.
    D. Popular sentiment in their countries was against them.

30. Which of the following served as secretary of war in the   30.___
    administration of Abraham Lincoln?
    A. Salmon P. Chase   B. Simon Cameron
    C. Caleb Smith   D. U.S. Grant

31. Approximately what percentage of Union forces throughout   31.___
    the war were volunteers?
    A. 35   B. 60   C. 75   D. 90

32. The main platform of the Know-Nothing Party, which rose   32.___
    to prominence in the 1850s, was centered on the issue of
    A. the secret role of the Society of Freemasons in public
       life
    B. taxation
    C. the abolition of slavery
    D. immigration and foreign settlement

33. During the period of military reconstruction, who was
    responsible for implementing the reconstruction of South
    Carolina?
    A. Daniel Sickles   B. John Pope
    C. John M. Schofield   D. Edward Ord

33.___

34. The primary unit in the Union's Regular army was the
    A. brigade   B. regiment   C. division   D. company

34.___

35. Which of the following battles is said to have opened the
    door to the mid-South for Union forces?
    A. Forts Henry and Donelson
    B. Murfreesboro
    C. Shiloh
    D. Vicksburg

35.___

36. In January of 1861, the flag of the *Pacific Republic* was
    raised in
    A. Astoria, by Oregon neutralists
    B. San Francisco, by pro-Union Californians
    C. San Diego, by defectors from the Union Navy
    D. Stockton, by pro-Confederate Californians

36.___

37. Which of the following Southern states was NOT subjected
    to military reconstruction after the war?
    A. Arkansas   B. Virginia
    C. Tennessee   D. North Carolina

37.___

38. Who commanded the Union Army of the James in the failed
    Bermuda Hundred campaign of 1864?
    A. Henry Halleck   B. Benjamin Butler
    C. George Gordon Meade   D. George McClellan

38.___

39. The sharecropping system that arose in the South after the
    Civil War had the effect of
    I. the replacement of factors with bankers as sources
       for capital
    II. the increasing Southern reliance on a limited number
        of crops
    III. a loss of control for the planter over the purchasing
         process

    The CORRECT answer is:
    A. I *only*   B. I, III   C. II *only*   D. I, II, III

39.___

40. What was the term used throughout most of the war to
    denote slaves of indeterminate status who had been
    liberated by the military but could not yet be declared
    free?
    A. Foragers   B. Collaterals
    C. Spoils   D. Contrabands

40.___

41. In all of the antebellum South, by far the majority of   41.___
    Southerners were
    A. slaves   B. poor whites
    C. rich planters   D. small farmers

42. Each of the following cities was an important link in the   42.___
    Underground Railroad during the 1850s EXCEPT
    A. Pittsburgh   B. Chicago
    C. Columbus   D. Detroit

43. The corps known as Berdan's Sharpshooters made their   43.___
    greatest contribution to the Union military effort by
    protecting the Federal flank at the battle of
    A. Second Bull Run   B. Antietam
    C. Gettysburg   D. Shiloh

44. General Lee's goals for his Antietam Campaign included   44.___
      I. winning over the border states
     II. encouraging foreign intervention
    III. plowing a route to Washington

    The CORRECT answer is:
    A. I *only*   B. I, II   C. III *only*   D. II, III

45. What was the nickname given to the foragers who accom-   45.___
    panied General William T. Sherman during his march to the
    sea and Carolinas campaign?
    A. Clinkers   B. Idlers
    C. Scroungers   D. Bummers

46. The value of United States *greenbacks* issued during the   46.___
    war was determined by
    A. the nation's credit   B. the British pound
    C. bond sales   D. the gold standard

47. The first Confederate invasion of the New Mexico territory   47.___
    was undertaken in 1861 as an ostensible *buffalo hunt*, led
    by
    A. Henry H. Sibley   B. John Robert Baylor
    C. Isaac Lynde   D. Sam Houston

48. In 1866, President Johnson vetoed a bill that would have   48.___
    renewed the authority of the Freedmen's Bureau. His
    primary reason for doing this was that
    A. freedmen were already being granted adequate protec-
       tion under the new state governments
    B. it would constitute an unwarranted continuance of a
       war power in a time of peace
    C. it would have given too much power to his political
       adversaries in Congress
    D. freedmen were too susceptible to exploitation by
       officers

49. The *carpetbaggers* who occupied the South during and after   49.___
the Civil War were most disproportionately numerous in
the state of
    A. Arkansas   B. Alabama   C. Louisiana D. Mississippi

50. Which of the following was NOT a founding member of the   50.___
American Anti-Slavery Society?
    A. James G. Birney   B. Elijah Lovejoy
    C. Lewis Tappan   D. Theodore D. Weld

KEY (CORRECT ANSWERS)

1. A	11. D	21. B	31. D	41. D
2. B	12. D	22. D	32. D	42. A
3. C	13. D	23. A	33. A	43. C
4. C	14. C	24. B	34. D	44. B
5. A	15. D	25. B	35. A	45. D
6. D	16. C	26. C	36. D	46. A
7. B	17. A	27. B	37. C	47. B
8. D	18. A	28. D	38. B	48. B
9. B	19. B	29. D	39. D	49. D
10. B	20. B	30. B	40. D	50. B

EXAMINATION SECTION
TEST 1

Directions: Each question or incomplete statement is followed by several suggested answers or completions. Select the one that BEST answers the question or completes the statement. *PRINT THE LETTER OF THE CORRECT ANSWER IN THE SPACE AT THE RIGHT.*

1) President Lincoln's reluctance to emancipate slaves in the first two years of the Civil War can most clearly be attributed to his

1. _____

    A.   uncertainty about the morality of slavery
    B.   desire to retain the loyalty of border states
    C.   uncertainty about the constitutionality of slavery
    D.   fear of British and French intervention in the war

2) Southern demands that slavery be allowed to expand into the western territories seems to have been motivated largely by the

2. _____

    A.   profiteering machinations of powerful agricultural interests
    B.   desire for a wider market for surplus slaves
    C.   fear that free territories would become breeding grounds for abolitionist agitators
    D.   doctrine of paternalism, which held that slavery actually protected blacks

3) The Civil Rights Act of 1866, passed over President Johnson's veto, granted African-Americans the right to

3. _____

    I.   make contracts
    II.   own land and private property
    III.   sue
    IV.   vote

    A.   I only
    B.   I, II and III
    C.   III only
    D.   I, II, III and IV

4) The Union victory that essentially split the Confederacy in half occurred at

4. _____

    A.   Atlanta
    B.   Antietam
    C.   Vicksburg
    D.   Chattanooga

5)   When Ulysses S. Grant was made General-in-Chief of the Union armed forces, he

    I.   abolished the exchange of prisoners
    II.   concentrated Union forces in the West
    III.   pressed southward after the battle of the Wilderness
    IV.   decided upon a "war of attrition" strategy that was sure to produce many Union casualties

A.   I and II
B.   I, III and IV
C.   III and IV
D.   I, II, III and IV

5. _____

6)   The term "Solid South" was applied to the former Confederate States after Reconstruction because these states

A.   passed a number of Jim Crow laws
B.   exhibited a culture that proved to be impenetrable to outsiders
C.   turned increasingly toward an industrial economy
D.   consistently voted Democratic

6. _____

7)   The Compromise of 1850 was approved by President

A.   James K. Polk
B.   Franklin Pierce
C.   Millard Fillmore
D.   Zachary Taylor

7. _____

8)   Which of the following Union generals declared in 1862 that slaves in the states of Georgia, South Carolina, and Florida were free by virtue of the states' subjection to martial law—only to have the order promptly rescinded by President Lincoln?

A.   Philip Sheridan
B.   Benjamin Butler
C.   George Armstrong Custer
D.   David Hunter

8. _____

9)   In the first 25 years of the 19th century, the event that had the greatest impact on the institution of slavery was the

A.   increasing domestic demand for cotton from textile manufacturers
B.   invention of the cotton gin
C.   use of more repressive means of discipline
D.   introduction of crop rotation and fertilizers

9. _____

10) "Fire-Eaters" were   10. _____

A.   extreme abolitionists who, like John Brown, advocated emancipation through violence
B.   Northern politicians who traveled South to make their fortune during Reconstruction
C.   extremist pro-slavery politicians from the South
D.   Union Navy personnel who took on the dangerous job of loading on-board cannons with balls and shot

11)   Which of the following parties, in the decade before the Civil War,   11. _____
generally supported Western expansion, a strong federal government, and the
abolition of slavery?

A.   Democratic
B.   Know-Nothing
C.   Republican
D.   Free Soil

12)   The overarching intent of Union General Winfield Scott's "Anaconda   12. _____
Plan" was to win the war

A.   rapidly by capturing the Confederate capital
B.   by draining escaped slaves away from the South and putting them to work
C.   with minimal bloodshed
D.   by ruining the South's capability to fight

13)   Each of the following battles was a part of the Overland Campaign,   13. _____
EXCEPT

A.   Cold Harbor
B.   Gettysburg
C.   Wilson's Wharf
D.   Spotsylvania

14)   As president, James Buchanan urged that the issues related to slavery   14. _____
in the territories should be decided by

A.   armed conflict
B.   a national referendum
C.   the Supreme Court
D.   popular sovereignty

15) The Militia Act of 1862 decreed that all freed slaves could 15. _____

A. enlist in the Union military service, but only as laborers, not as soldiers.
B. be drafted in the Union military service, but would only perform labor.
C. enlist in the Union military service and move up the ranks through promotion, like any other soldier
D. enlist in the Union military service but not serve as officers in any capacity

16) Juneteenth is an official holiday, celebrated in more than a dozen U.S. states, that commemorates the announcement of the abolition of slavery in 16. _____

A. Georgia
B. Mississippi
C. Florida
D. Texas

17) The "fifth border state," carved out of pro-union slave territory, was 17. _____

A. Delaware
B. West Virginia
C. Indiana
D. Tennessee

18) The Radical Republicans' extension of the vote to freedmen in the Southern states was 18. _____

A. granted because without black suffrage, the states would not ratify the Fourteenth Amendment
B. widely perceived as a cynical ploy to secure millions of voters as Republicans for years to come
C. from the beginning, one of the most basic requirements of a Southern state's readmission to the Union
D. an attempt to stave off the effects of the "black codes"

19) The _____ Amendment to the Constitution provides equality before the law and citizenship rights to African-Americans. 19. _____

A. Twelfth
B. Thirteenth
C. Fourteenth
D. Fifteenth

20) One important reason that the Radical Republicans began to lose power was that

20. _____

A. Southern states were not making any substantial progress toward providing civil liberties for freed slaves
B. they suffered from internal squabbles that divided their political strength
C. many Northerners lost interest in changing the South
D. they opposed the imperial expansion of U.S. power overseas, which was becoming an increasingly popular idea

21) The Confederate general who advocated the establishment of permanent "entrenched" lines of defense against Union invasion, and who thus presaged the advent of trench warfare, was

21. _____

A. Thomas J. "Stonewall" Jackson
B. Robert E. Lee
C. J.E.B. Stuart
D. Braxton Bragg

22) The primary reason for the exclusion of free blacks from the Union Army during the early stages of the Civil War was that

22. _____

A. most Northerners were opposed to blacks serving in the Army
B. most white soldiers refused to serve with blacks
C. it was against federal law to arm black people
D. at the time, the North already had sufficient troops

23) During the Civil War, the Union objective that proved to be the most difficult, and which took the longest to achieve, was the

23. _____

A. naval blockade of Southern ports
B. control of Mississippi River traffic
C. capture of New Orleans
D. capture of Richmond

24) The position of most American black leaders regarding the resettlement plan proposed by the American Colonization Society in the early 19th century was that they were

24. _____

A. opposed to it because they felt attached to the United States
B. opposed to it because they considered it a scheme to deport free blacks
C. in favor of it because ex-slaves would receive both land and material provisions
D. in favor of it because ex-slaves would finally have the right to self-determination

25) U.S. territories that sided with the Confederacy during the Civil War   25. _____
included

       I.   Montana
       II.   Colorado
       III.   Indian Territory (Oklahoma)
       IV.   New Mexico

A.   I and II
B.   I and III
C.   III and IV
D.   None of the above

KEY (CORRECT ANSWERS)

1. B
2. C
3. B
4. C
5. B

6. D
7. C
8. D
9. B
10. C

11. C
12. C
13. B
14. C
15. A

16. D
17. B
18. A
19. C
20. C

21. B
22. C
23. D
24. B
25. C

TEST 2

Directions: Each question or incomplete statement is followed by several suggested answers or completions. Select the one that BEST answers the question or completes the statement. *PRINT THE LETTER OF THE CORRECT ANSWER IN THE SPACE AT THE RIGHT.*

1)   President Lincoln's justification for the Civil War could best be summed up by the statement that

      1. _____

A.   the Northern states were entitled share the resources of Southern states
B.   he was an abolitionist who wanted to end slavery in the United States
C.   his oath of office required that he work to defend and preserve the Union
D.   his constitutional authority required that he punish rebellion

2)   What was the post-Reconstruction case in which the U.S. Supreme Court ruled that "separate but equal" public facilities for black and white Americans were lawful?

      2. _____

A.   *Plessy v. Ferguson*
B.   *Giles v. Harris*
C.   *Dred Scott v. Sandford*
D.   *Civil Rights Cases (1883)*

3)   The Free Soil Party was formed in the United States largely as a faction in support of the

      3. _____

A.   Missouri Compromise
B.   Wilmot Proviso
C.   Kansas-Nebraska Act
D.   Emancipation Proclamation

4)   The Compromise of 1850 could most accurately be described as a series of laws that were intended to

      4. _____

A.   clarify some of the vagueness inherent in the doctrine of "popular sovereignty"
B.   increase Northern political control over the western territories
C.   stem the violence in "Bleeding Kansas"
D.   resolve sectional and territorial issues arising from the Mexican-American War

5)   Which of the following occurred FIRST?   5. _____

A.   Peninsula campaign (March-July 1862)
B.   Siege of Petersburg
C.   Gettysburg
D.   Chickamauga

6)   How many slave uprisings in the antebellum South resulted in the   6. _____
death of whites?

A.   1
B.   2
C.   4
D.   7

7)   President Lincoln's plan for Reconstruction required Southern states to   7. _____

   I.   guarantee suffrage for blacks
   II.   adopt a republican form of government
   III.   require some Southerners to take an oath of loyalty to the
          Union
   IV.   accept the abolition of slavery

A.   I and IV
B.   IV only
C.   II, III and IV
D.   I, II, III and IV

8)   The _____ was an overt statement that Afri-   8. _____
can-Americans could never be citizens of the United States.

A.   *Dred Scott* decision
B.   Compromise of 1820
C.   Lecompton Constitution
D.   Fugitive Slave Law

9)   During the first half of the 19th century, the most divisive and contro-   9. _____
versial issue regarding slavery was the status of

A.   the international slave trade
B.   slavery in the District of Columbia
C.   slavery in the western territories
D.   fugitive slaves

10)	The most strategically important location to be captured by the Union	10. _____
Navy during the first year of the war was

A.	New Orleans
B.	Savannah
C.	Port Royal
D.	Wilmington

11)	Which of the following black abolitionists was arguably the first	11. _____
proponent of American black nationalism and the first African American field
officer in the U.S. Army?

A.	Martin Delaney
B.	David Walker
C.	Frederick Douglass
D.	Elijah Lovejoy

12)	For blacks who fled the South during the Reconstruction Era, the two	12. _____
most likely destinations were:

A.	New York (Harlem) and Philadelphia
B.	Detroit and Chicago
C.	Canada and Cuba
D.	Kansas and Liberia

13)	The name given those settlers in Kansas Territory during the 1850s	13. _____
"Bleeding Kansas" era who opposed the extension of slavery into Kansas was

A.	Jayhawkers
B.	Leavenworths
C.	Free Staters
D.	Thayerites

14)	The National Union Party came to an end when	14. _____

A.	George McClellan was defeated
B.	Abraham Lincoln was assassinated
C.	Ulysses S. Grant was elected president
D.	Andrew Johnson's term ended

15)	Men who enlisted in the Union Army in 1861 signed up for a period of	15. _____

A.	eight months
B.	one year
C.	eighteen months
D.	three years

16) By 1860, _____, which had no railroads in 1850, had twelve lines running through it.

16. _____

A. New York City
B. Columbus
C. Chicago
D. Kansas City

17) At the outset of the Civil War, the North had a numerical advantage over the South in each of the following, EXCEPT

17. _____

A. taxable wealth
B. West Point graduates
C. existing capital
D. industrial capacity

18) During the Civil War, Winston County, in the state of _____ refused to join the Confederacy and declared itself the Republic of Winston.

18. _____

A. Missouri
B. Alabama
C. Virginia
D. Florida

19) President Andrew Johnson's narrow avoidance of conviction on impeachment charges was largely due to

19. _____

A. several compromises worked out in secret to appease the Radical Republican faction that sought his removal
B. his agreement to backtrack and reappoint his secretary of war
C. the reluctance of some Republicans to use impeachment as a political weapon against the presidency
D. the moral authority he carried as Abraham Lincoln's choice for the vice presidency

20) Which of the following, killed relatively early in the Civil War at Shiloh, was considered by Jefferson Davis to be the finest general in the Confederacy?

20. _____

A. J.E.B. Stuart
B. Albert Sidney Johnston
C. Braxton Bragg
D. Thomas J. "Stonewall" Jackson

21)   Slavery was abolished in the United States by the _____   21. _____
Amendment to the Constitution.

A.   Twelfth
B.   Thirteenth
C.   Fourteenth
D.   Fifteenth

22)   *I am not now, nor ever have been in favor of bringing about in any*   22. _____
way the social or political equality of the white and black races. I am not
now nor ever have been in favor of making voters or jurors of Negroes, nor of
qualifying them to hold office, nor of intermarriages with white people. There
is a physical difference between the white and the black races which will for-
ever forbid the two races living together on social or political equality. There
must be a position of superior and inferior, and I am in favor of assigning the
superior position to the white man.

The words above were spoken in 1858 by

A.   Jefferson Davis
B.   Abraham Lincoln
C.   John C. Calhoun
D.   Stephen A. Douglas

23)   During the Civil War the North experienced several riots sparked by   23. _____
the issue of _____; and the South suffered riots over the issue of

_____.

A.   slavery; secession
B.   popular sovereignty; the enlistment of blacks in the Confederate Army
C.   British meddling; the fugitive slave laws
D.   the military draft; food

24)   During the Civil War, Great Britain and France generally   24. _____

A.   saw advantages in a divided United States, but pursued cautious poli-
cies toward both sides
B.   favored permanent separation, but openly supported the North
C.   supported the South, despite their opposition to slavery, because of
their dependence on Southern cotton
D.   had no interest in the outcome of the conflict

25)   Regarding free black people in the antebellum United States,   25. _____

      I.   most preferred to live in cities
      II.   some owned property, and a few owned slaves
      III.   some who owned property could vote
      IV.   some were kidnapped and sold into slavery in another state

A.   I only
B.   I, II and IV
C.   II and III
D.   I, II, III and IV

———

KEY (CORRECT ANSWERS)

1. C
2. A
3. B
4. D
5. A

6. A
7. C
8. A
9. C
10. C

11. A
12. D
13. C
14. D
15. D

16. A
17. B
18. B
19. C
20. B

21. B
22. B
23. D
24. A
25. B

TEST 3

Directions: Each question or incomplete statement is followed by several suggested answers or completions. Select the one that BEST answers the question or completes the statement. *PRINT THE LETTER OF THE CORRECT ANSWER IN THE SPACE AT THE RIGHT.*

1) What was the term used for pro-Union guerilla fighters in the Kansas Territory during the Civil War?

1. _____

A. Jayhawkers
B. Bushwhackers
C. Butternuts
D. Hedge-apples

2) General Benjamin Butler's insistence that escaped slaves should be freed was based on the

2. _____

A. dire shortage of Union troops, which could be alleviated by the use of black troops
B. principle that slavery was a moral evil
C. unsolvable question of whether they were slaves or kidnapped free blacks
D. fact that once returned to their masters, they were effectively aiding the Confederacy

3) Pickett's Charge, the infamous assault ordered by General Robert E. Lee that killed more than half the Confederate troops who carried it out, occurred at the Battle of

3. _____

A. Gettysburg
B. Chancellorsville
C. Antietam
D. Spotsylvania

4) The Reconstruction proposal offered by Andrew Johnson included each of the following, EXCEPT

4. _____

A. full civil and political equality for freed blacks
B. allowing Southern states to adopt special legal codes
C. increasing the number of Democrats in Congress
D. allowing former Confederate officials to hold office

5)   Which of the following events occurred LAST?   5. _____

A.   Compromise of 1850
B.   Crittenden Compromise
C.   Firing on Fort Sumter
D.   Crittenden-Johnson Resolution

6)   The *Dred Scott* decision seemed to indicate that   6. _____

A.   the Constitution's position of slavery was clear
B.   most Supreme Court justices sympathized with the South
C.   most Supreme Court justices had become impatient with the issue of slavery and wanted it to become more settled
D.   the American press generally supported slavery

7)   The election of 1860 resulted in each of the following, EXCEPT   7. _____

A.   the Democratic Party dividing into feuding Northern and Southern wings
B.   the splintering of the Republican Party over the issue of slavery
C.   the President of the United States had virtually no support in the South
D.   an election winner who was chosen by less than half the population

8)   Most northerners who voiced opposition to the extension of slavery into the western territories did so on the grounds that   8. _____

A.   slavery was immoral
B.   free workers would be forced to compete with slaves for jobs
C.   it would create a sectional imbalance in the legislature
D.   slavery inevitably ushered in higher taxes and a more regulated economy

9)   The only major candidate in the election of 1860 who seemed to believe that secession was a real possibility was   9. _____

A.   William Seward
B.   Abraham Lincoln
C.   John Bell
D.   Stephen Douglas

10. _____

10)   The Union advance to Vicksburg was enabled by the victory at

A.   Shiloh
B.   Jackson
C.   Antietam
D.   New Orleans

11) Southern whites who supported Reconstruction in the South were typically referred to as

11. _____

A. Fire-Eaters
B. redeemers
C. carpetbaggers
D. scalawags

12) The short-lived Know-Nothing Party was promptly undone by the issue of _____ and disappeared from American politics.

12. _____

A. immigration
B. slavery
C. federal funding for internal improvements
D. temperance

13) The Union Victory at _____ was strategically important because it secured control of the entire Mississippi River.

13. _____

A. Hannibal
B. Memphis
C. New Orleans
D. Vicksburg

14) Of the following, the event that occurred FIRST was

14. _____

A. The enactment of the Fugitive Slave Law
B. The formation of the Liberty Party
C. William Lloyd Garrison's publication of *The Liberator*
D. The Compromise of 1850

15) The use of slave labor in colonial Virginia

15. _____

A. fulfilled the original plan of the Virginia Company
B. spread rapidly as blacks displaced white indentured servants
C. was forced onto reluctant Virginians by English merchants and the Crown
D. was the first instance of European enslavement of Africans

16) The percentage of Southern officeholders who were African-American during the Reconstruction era was about

16. _____

A. 5
B. 20
C. 45
D. 60

17)   Southern support for the Compromise of 1850 was based primarily on its provision for

17. _____

A.   an equal number of free and slave states
B.   the possibility of Texas being divided into five separate states
C.   slavery in all newly acquired territories
D.   the return of fugitive slaves

18)   Each of the following battles was a victory for General Ulysses S. Grant, EXCEPT

18. _____

A.   Chickamauga
B.   Shiloh
C.   Chattanooga
D.   Fort Donelson

19)   The Civil Rights Act of 1866 was vetoed by President Andrew Johnson on the grounds that it

19. _____

A.   would operate in favor of the black race and against the white race
B.   would further divide Northern and Southern states
C.   was unconstitutional
D.   did not go far enough in granting civil liberties to freed slaves

20)   Ultimately, the legislative battle over the impeachment of President Andrew Johnson was fought over the constitutional principle of

20. _____

A.   the "three-fifths" rule
B.   separation of powers
C.   interstate commerce
D.   free speech and assembly

21)   In 1852, Whig candidate Winfield Scott

21. _____

A.   urged the Supreme Court to settle the issue of slavery once and for all
B.   would likely have won the election if he hadn't supported a high tariff
C.   ran on a platform that called for popular sovereignty in the territories
D.   alienated Southern voters by aligning himself with Northern anti-slavery leaders

22) The constitution that finally settled the issue of slavery in Kansas was   22. _____
the _____ Constitution, adopted in 1858 and establishing it
as a free state

A.   Topeka
B.   Leavenworth
C.   Wyandotte
D.   Lecompton

23) Radical and moderate Republicans united in opposition to President   23. _____
Andrew Johnson after his

A.   dismissal of Secretary of War Edwin Stanton
B.   vetoes of the Freedmen's Bureau bill and the Civil Rights Act
C.   refusal to deviate from Abraham Lincoln's plan for Reconstruction
D.   proposal for a federal agency to provide relief, food and medical care
to poor white Southerners

24) The 1858 Lincoln-Douglas debates for the Senate seat from Illinois   24. _____
focused primarily on the issue of

A.   states' rights
B.   monetary policy
C.   slavery
D.   tariffs

25) The newly formed Republican Party achieved rapid prosperity   25. _____

A.   with its first national ticket
B.   because of its advocacy of popular sovereignty in the territories
C.   because of outrage over "Bleeding Kansas" and the caning of Senator
Charles Sumner
D.   in the South in the elections of 1854

KEY (CORRECT ANSWERS)

1. A
2. D
3. A
4. A
5. D

6. B
7. B
8. B
9. D
10. A

11. D
12. B
13. D
14. C
15. B

16. B
17. D
18. A
19. A
20. B

21. D
22. C
23. C
24. C
25. C

TEST 4

Directions: Each question or incomplete statement is followed by several suggested answers or completions. Select the one that BEST answers the question or completes the statement. *PRINT THE LETTER OF THE CORRECT ANSWER IN THE SPACE AT THE RIGHT.*

1) Which of the following was NOT a tactic used by abolitionists before the Civil War?

1. _____

A. Requesting that Congress pass laws outlawing slavery in the states
B. Providing assistance to escaped slaves
C. Appealing to the morality and conscience of slaveholders
D. Lobbying state legislatures to pass personal liberty laws

2) One direct result of the Fourteenth Amendment was that

A. former slaves were given allotments of land by the federal government
2. _____
B. Southern states began to enact Jim Crow laws
C. the Reconstruction Era had effectively come to an end
D. the guarantees contained in the Bill of Rights were applied to all state actions

3) President Buchanan considered the Lecompton Constitution to be a

3. _____

A. fundamentally flawed document that had no constitutional foundation
B. violation of the principle of popular sovereignty
C. sign that secession was imminent
D. fairly moderate compromise that deserved to be adopted

4) The Reconstruction-era political coalition known as the "Redeemers" was composed mostly of

4. _____

A. Bourbon Democrats
B. carpetbaggers
C. copperheads
D. scalawags

5) The _____ Party, formed in 1860, was made up of conservative Whigs who wanted to preserve the Union.

5. _____

A. Constitutional Union
B. Free Soil
C. Northern Democratic
D. Know-Nothing

6) Which of the following occurred LAST?   6. _____

A. Veto of Freedmen's Bureau extension
B. Lincoln assassination
C. Military Reconstruction Acts
D. Johnson impeachment

7) The Union Army expedition in the Mississippi Campaign was com-   7. _____
manded by each of the following, EXCEPT

A. Benjamin Butler
B. Henry Halleck
C. Nathaniel P. Banks
D. Ulysses S. Grant

8) The Reconstruction Acts of 1867 applied to every Southern state ex- 8. _____
cept _____, which had ratified the Fourteenth Amendment.

A. Alabama
B. Virginia
C. Texas
D. Tennessee

9) Ulysses S. Grant's main competition for the presidency in the election 9. _____
of 1872 was

A. Thomas Andrews Hendricks
B. Rutherford B. Hayes
C. William McKinley
D. Horace Greeley

10) During the Civil War, Republicans enacted each of the following, EX- 10. _____
CEPT

A. land grants for railroad construction
B. a low tariff to encourage free trade
C. a national banking system
D. free land to homesteaders

11) The Whig Party was essentially destroyed by the   11. _____

A. Kansas-Nebraska Act
B. election of Abraham Lincoln
C. annexation of Texas
D. Missouri Compromise

12) The North effectively took control of the South's railroad network with the 1864 capture of

12. _____

A. Gettysburg
B. Vicksburg
C. Birmingham
D. Atlanta

13) A white Southerner would be legally exempted from military duty if he

13. _____

A. filed for conscientious objector status
B. received an educational deferment
C. owned at least 20 slaves
D. could prove he was the sole means of support for his dependents

14) Black politicians of the Reconstruction era tended to believe that

14. _____

A. none of the white race could be trusted
B. it was only possible to work with Northern whites
C. blacks and Southern whites would have to find a way to work together
D. the only way for blacks to be safe was to establish isolated home-rule communities

15) The Union occupation of New Orleans was administered by

15. _____

A. David Farragut
B. William Jennings Bryan
C. Benjamin Butler
D. Nathaniel P. Banks

16) The anti-abolitionist riots, also known as the Farren Riots, occurred in 1934 in the city of

16. _____

A. Richmond
B. New York
C. Charleston
D. Philadelphia

17) Each of the following states seceded in 1861, as a direct result of President Lincoln's call for Union troops, EXCEPT

17. _____

A. Tennessee
B. Texas
C. Virginia
D. Arkansas

18) *There are few, I believe, in this enlightened age, who will not acknowledge that slavery as an institution is a moral and political evil.*

The words above were written by

A. Alexander Stephens
B. John C. Calhoun
C. Robert E. Lee
D. Abraham Lincoln

18. _____

19) By the end of the first year of the Civil War, inflation in the Confederacy had reached a rate of _____ per month.

A. 1
B. 5
C. 12
D. 23

19. _____

20) Which of the following NOT was a border state during the Civil War?

A. Maryland
B. Missouri
C. West Virginia
D. Tennessee

20. _____

21) The Democratic nominee for president in the 1848 was a major proponent of popular sovereignty named

A. Zachary Taylor
B. George Dallas
C. James K. Polk
D. Lewis Cass

21. _____

22) The pro-slavery guerillas who harassed the abolitionist settlements in "Bleeding Kansas" were known as

A. Sunflowers
B. Border Ruffians
C. the James Gang
D. Jayhawkers

22. _____

23) The first major military clash of the Civil War occurred at

23. _____

A. Fort Sumter
B. Stones River (Murfreesboro)
C. Bull Run (Manassas)
D. Gettysburg

24) Which of the following parties, in the decade before the Civil War, generally supported Western expansion, popular sovereignty, and states' rights?

24. _____

A. Democratic
B. Republican
C. Free Soil
D. Whig

25) Which of the following terms was NOT commonly used to denote Northern Democrats who wanted to make peace with the South?

25. _____

A. Know-Nothings
B. Copperheads
C. Bushwhackers
D. Butternuts

KEY (CORRECT ANSWERS)

1. A
2. D
3. D
4. A
5. A

6. D
7. A
8. D
9. D
10. B

11. A
12. D
13. C
14. C
15. C

16. B
17. B
18. C
19. C
20. D

21. D
22. B
23. C
24. A
25. B

EXAMINATION SECTION
TEST 1

Directions: Each question or incomplete statement is followed by several suggested answers or completions. Select the one that BEST answers the question or completes the statement. *PRINT THE LETTER OF THE CORRECT ANSWER IN THE SPACE AT THE RIGHT.*

1)   Sectional differences developed in the United States largely as a result of

A.   economic conditions and interests
B.   foreign subversion, especially on the part of Great Britain and France
C.   differences in ethnic and cultural patterns of settlement and migration
D.   the federal government's willingness to defer to the doctrine of states' rights

1. _____

2)   The three-day Battle of _____ effectively saved the Union and permanently changed the course of the Civil War.

A.   Vicksburg
B.   Atlanta
C.   Shiloh
D.   Gettysburg

2. _____

3)   By far, most of the military engagements between the North and the South during the Civil War took place in

A.   Tennessee
B.   Georgia
C.   South Carolina
D.   Virginia

3. _____

4)   The poll taxes and literacy tests, and segregated facilities that were legally implemented in Southern states beginning in the post-Reconstruction era were examples of

A.   Jim Crow laws
B.   fugitive slave laws
C.   Black Codes
D.   civil rights laws

4. _____

5)   The Military Reconstruction Act of 1867 provided for   5. _____

        I.   black suffrage in all Southern states
        II.   the denial of suffrage to former Confederate officials and mili
                tary officers
        III.   military rule of the South
        IV.   a ban on poll taxes and literacy tests

A.   I and II
B.   I, II and III
C.   II, III and IV
D.   I, II, II! and IV

6)   Jefferson Davis's fundamental problem in leading the Confederate   6. _____
States of America was that

A.   in order to lead effectively, he had to seek more centralized authority
over a society that valued states' rights
B.   the war required a rapid mobilization that could not be conducted successfully in the South, because the infrastructure was so poorly conceived and
maintained
C.   there were not enough young Southern men dedicated to the cause of
the Confederacy
D.   he was a lofty, ideological thinker in a society that needed quick, pragmatic answers to mostly military questions

7)   Fort Henry's strategic important was that it protected the   7. _____

A.   Mobile Bay
B.   Ohio River Valley
C.   Bilox: Harbor
D.   Tennessee River

8)   The Wilmot Proviso, if passed in 1846, would have   8. _____

A.   left the issue of slavery in any territory acquired as a result of the
Mexican War to be decided by popular sovereignty
B.   permitted slavery in any territory acquired as a result of the Mexican
War
C.   banned slavery in any territory acquired as a result of the Mexican War
D.   banned slavery in all existing U.S. territories

9)   Abraham Lincoln's military strategy could best be described as a(n)   9. _____

A.   quick strike at the capital of Richmond that would precipitate the fall of the Confederacy
B.   grinding push to "clear and hold" the major urban centers
C.   two-front strategy that would keep pressure on Richmond while advancing in the Mississippi Valley
D.   "Anaconda Plan" of slowly starving the South into submission

10)   The two Southern counties won by Lincoln during the 1860 election   10. _____
were in the state of

A.   Alabama
B.   Missouri
C.   Maryland
D.   Tennessee

11)   The "Seven Days Battles" were fought in 1862 near   11. _____

A.   Vicksburg
B.   Richmond
C.   Atlanta
D.   the Shenandoah Valley

12)   The American Anti-Slavery Society was officially formed in   12. _____

A.   1789
B.   1804
C.   1833
D.   1840

13)   Specifically, the Freeport Doctrine argued that   13. _____

A.   slavery could be prevented from any territory by the refusal of the people living in that territory to pass laws favorable to slavery
B.   slavery could not legally be extended into the territories
C.   the issue of slavery in the territories should be decided by popular sovereignty
D.   the international slave trade would soon die out if it were unregulated

14)   Initially, the Emancipation Proclamation affected   14. _____

A.   about 4 million slaves in the border states
B.   all slaves in the states that were loyal to the Union
C.   only those slaves that had already escaped to the Union side
D.   only those slaves whose freedom had been purchased by abolitionist activists

15) Southern Whigs' support of Zachary Taylor for the presidency in 1848 was due to his

15. _____

A. espousal of the doctrine of popular sovereignty
B. support of the expansion of slavery into the territories
C. outstanding record as a military hero during the Mexican-American War
D. vocal support of the institution of slavery

16) The main reason that manufacturing in the South lagged behind that of the North was because

16. _____

A. white Southerners tended to look down on manufacturing jobs
B. Southerners were generally less educated
C. slave labor and industry were seen as incompatible
D. cotton was more profitable

17) During the first year of the Civil War, about _____ percent of Confederate ships were able to penetrate the Union blockade.

17. _____

A. 90
B. 65
C. 35
D. 10

18) In order to provide a haven for freed slaves during Reconstruction, President Ulysses S. Grant attempted to

18. _____

A. create legislation that would offer freedmen more favorable home-steading terms than whites
B. elevate the Freedmen's Bureau to cabinet status
C. set aside the recently unorganized territory of the Red River Valley as a "blacks only" settlement
D. annex the Dominican Republic

19) During the Civil War, the South suffered shortages of each of the following, EXCEPT

19. _____

A. munitions
B. food
C. soldiers
D. transportation facilities

20) Virginia's main pre-Civil War crop was   20. _____

A.   tobacco
B.   hemp
C.   sugar
D.   cotton

21) Before the Civil War, abolitionists were generally unpopular among   21. _____
Northern business owners, because

A.   many Northern businesses depended on cotton from the South
B.   in their opinion, slaves were treated better than most Northern workers
C.   many Northerners still owned slaves who worked in factories
D.   the attacks and demonstrations by abolitionists tended to be violent
and indiscriminate and often targeted business establishments

22) Which of the following cities was captured the day after the Battle of   22. _____
Gettysburg?

A.   Atlanta
B.   Fredericksburg
C.   Vicksburg
D.   Nashville

23) In the South, and especially Virginia, the Nat Turner rebellion and the   23. _____
publication of *The Liberator* had the effect of

A.   dividing Southerners among three clear-cut factions of abolitionists,
moderates, and pro-slavery advocates
B.   encouraging state legislatures to discuss the issue of abolition in Con-
gress
C.   galvanizing continued support for slavery
D.   encouraging the migration of slaves to the Midwest.

24) In 1858, when future President Abraham Lincoln said, "A house di-   24. _____
vided cannot stand," he indicated his belief that

A.   secession of the Southern states would be the most peaceful solution to
the problem of slavery
B.   he intended to invade the South and free the slaves
C.   there should be a separate representative legislature for the South
D.   the nation could no longer exist as half slave and half free

25)   Earlier efforts to settle the issue of slavery were frustrated in the 1840s   25. _____
and 1850s largely because

A.   the nation was expanding rapidly westward
B.   political parties were seizing on the issue as a "wedge" to divide the
electorate and force them into political affiliations
C.   the Southern economy was nearing a collapse
D.   the British and French governments were sending agitators to the
South

KEY (CORRECT ANSWERS)

1. A
2. D
3. D
4. A
5. B

6. A
7. D
8. C
9. C
10. B

11. B
12. C
13. A
14. C
15. B

16. D
17. A
18. D
19. A
20. A

21. A
22. C
23. C
24. D
25. A

TEST 2

Directions: Each question or incomplete statement is followed by several suggested answers or completions. Select the one that BEST answers the question or completes the statement. *PRINT THE LETTER OF THE CORRECT ANSWER IN THE SPACE AT THE RIGHT.*

1)   The _____ created a line at 36°30'N to divide future slave and free territories and states in the United States.

1. _____

A.   Missouri Compromise of 1820
B.   Compromise of 1850
C.   Fugitive Slave Act of 1850
D.   Kansas-Nebraska Act of 1854

2)   Of the four proposed constitutions for the new state of Kansas, the _____ Constitution supported the existence of slavery in the proposed state and protected rights of slaveholders.

2. _____

A.   Topeka
B.   Leavenworth
C.   Wyandotte
D.   Lecompton

3)   The Confederate cavalry was commanded by

3. _____

A.   J.E.B. Stuart
B.   Braxton Bragg
C.   Jubal Early
D.   P.G.T. Beauregard

4)   The limited success of the Union's early eastern campaigns are most often attributed to

4. _____

A.   the strategic brilliance of Confederate General
B.   George McClellan's overly cautious approach
C.   military genius of Robert E. Lee
D.   President Lincoln's constant interference in military matters

5. _____

5)   A major secessionist leader was

A.   Andrew Jackson
B.   William Yancey
C.   John Crittenden
D.   Robert E. Lee

6) In the United States, the principle of "popular sovereignty"   6. _____

    I.   was intended to be ambiguous
    II.   was interpreted differently by Northerners and Southerners
    III.   led to violence in the settlement of Kansas
    IV.   was first codified in the Compromise of 1850

A.   I only
B.   I and III
C.   II, III and IV
D.   I, II, III and IV

7) Each of the following Civil War battles took place in Virginia, EX-   7. _____
CEPT

A.   Gaines' Mill
B.   Bull Run
C.   Albemarle Sound
D.   Spotsylvania

8) Which of the following African-Americans called Reconstruction a   8. _____
"failure" because it did not follow through and reinforce the gains made by
blacks in terms of civil and political rights?

A.   Booker T. Washington
B.   Frederick Douglass
C.   W.E.B. DuBois
D.   Harriet Beecher Stowe

9) Lincoln's pocket veto of the Wade-Davis Bill was motivated primarily   9. _____
by his desire to

A.   marginalize the Radicals in shaping Reconstruction policy
B.   keep Jefferson Davis from grasping for power in the legislature
C.   preserve the delicate political coalitions that he had begun to construct
between northern and southern moderates
D.   ensure that Confederate leaders were properly punished for their role
in starting the Civil War

10) The new political party formed in 1854 was the _____   10. _____
Party.

A.   Bull Moose
B.   Know-Nothing
C.   Republican
D.   Free Soil

11)   The Pinckney Resolutions that were passed in Congress in 1835 and   11. _____
renewed substantially for several ensuing years resulted in

A.   a tenuous sectional balance in the Senate, but not the House
B.   a limited ability for state governments to regulate slavery
C.   the rise of the "Fire-Eaters" among representatives from Southern
states
D.   any petition regarding the issue of slavery to be tabled (neither read
nor discussed)

12)   The North tended to view the Reconstruction-era "black codes" as   12. _____

A.   evidence that the South was slowly allowing freed slaves to improve
their standing
B.   evidence that the South wanted to keep freed slaves economically
dependent and legally inferior
C.   a dangerous experiment in Southern social engineering that would lead
to the establishment of an extensive welfare state
D.   a pragmatic legislative solution to the problems posed in the South by
the sudden influx of freed slaves into civil society

13)   The "Peace Democrat" who was arrested and deported for treason by   13. _____
Abraham Lincoln was

A.   Daniel Voorhees
B.   Clement Vallandigham
C.   George McClellan
D.   Lambdin P. Milligan

14)   A major factor in the increasing prosperity of the United States during   14. _____
the early 1850s was

A.   widespread foreclosures
B.   high tariffs
C.   the increasing amount of gold in the economy
D.   easy credit and widespread land speculation

15)   President Andrew Johnson's plan for Reconstruction called for South-   15. _____
ern states to

A.   declare that their secessions were illegal
B.   grant suffrage to former slaves
C.   pay war reparations
D.   ratify the Fourteenth Amendment

16)   At the time the Emancipation Proclamation was issued, Lincoln's justi-   16. _____
fication for it was the

A.   Union's military advantage
B.   economic benefits it would bring to the North
C.   constitutional guarantees of personal liberty
D.   moral imperative of ending slavery

17)   Early in his presidency, Abraham Lincoln announced that the primary   17. _____
goal of his administration would be to

A.   abolish slavery throughout the country
B.   preserve the Union
C.   destroy the Southern plantation economy
D.   prevent slavery from extending into the western territories

18)   The Civil War battle that resulted in the greatest number of casualties   18. _____
was

A.   Gettysburg
B.   Chancellorsville
C.   Shiloh
D.   Antietam

19)   *This is to be a long war—very long— much longer than any politician*   19. _____
thinks.

The words above were written in 1861 by

A.   Jefferson Davis
B.   William T. Sherman
C.   Frederick Douglass
D.   Abraham Lincoln

20)   In January of 1862, Thaddeus Stevens, the Republican Leader in the   20. _____
House of Representatives, called for total war against the South, and argued
that emancipation

A.   would win valuable black recruits to the Union Army
B.   was a moral imperative
C.   was a necessary step that would win international support
D.   would ruin the Southern economy

21) During Reconstruction, Congressional blacks such as Hiram Revels 21. _____
and Blanche K. Bruce advocated strongly for citizenship and suffrage for Indians and Chinese immigrants because they

A. felt it was the only right thing to do, given their own record of persecution
B. had designs on reservation lands as a haven for freedmen
C. hoped to form a political alliance of "people of color"
D. wanted to strengthen the Republican Party

22) Each of the following was an element of the Radical Republican pro- 22. _____
gram implemented during Reconstruction, EXCEPT

A. the provision of 40 acres of land to each freedman
B. military occupation of the South
C. restrictions on presidential power
D. punishment of Confederate leaders

23) In publishing *The Impending Crisis of the South* in 1857, Hilton 23. _____
Rowan Helper attempted to

A. make the pragmatic argument that slavery actually harmed the Southern economy overall
B. warn Northerners that Southern states were prepared to secede over the issue of slavery
C. warn Southerners that the North was adopting an increasingly aggressive and militant posture, and invasion was imminent
D. make an impassioned plea against the cruelty and immorality of slavery

24) Many historians argue that the Compromise of 1850, while it did not 24. _____
settle the issue of slavery in the United States,

A. created a ten-year delay in which the South cashed in on its crops to build up a large surplus that effectively made the Civil War a longer and deadlier conflict than it might have been
B. created a ten-year delay in which the North rapidly industrialized and grew more capable of defeating the South in military conflict
C. was an effective means of dampening sectional divisions between North and South
D. effectively discouraged any foreign powers from interfering in the issue of slavery in the United States

25)   When George Henry White, the last Southern black of the post-Recon-   25. _____
struction period to serve in Congress, retired in _____, the U.S. Congress was completely white once again.

A.   1888
B.   1901
C.   1917
D.   1924

KEY (CORRECT ANSWERS)

1. A
2. D
3. A
4. B
5. B

6. D
7. C
8. C
9. C
10. C

11. D
12. B
13. B
14. C
15. A

16. A
17. B
18. A
19. B
20. D

21. D
22. A
23. A
24. B
25. B

TEST 3

Directions: Each question or incomplete statement is followed by several suggested answers or completions. Select the one that BEST answers the question or completes the statement. *PRINT THE LETTER OF THE CORRECT ANSWER IN THE SPACE AT THE RIGHT.*

1) In its Civil Rights Cases ruling of 1883, the Supreme Court ruled that   1. _____

   I.   the Thirteenth Amendment, while it outlawed the ownership of slaves, did not outlaw discriminatory behavior
   II.   the "equal protection" provision of the Fourteenth Amendment applied to government but not private individuals and organizations
   III.   "separate but equal" public facilities for black and white Americans were lawful
   IV.   the Civil Rights Act of 1875, which required open access to all public accommodations, whether publicly or privately owned, was unconstitutional

A.   I and II
B.   I, II and IV
C.   III only
D.   I, II, III and IV

2) The platform of the _____ Party during the   2. _____
1860 election was that the South had a constitutional right to slavery, but Congress should not allow it to expand.

A.   Constitutional Union
B.   Northern Democratic
C.   Southern Democratic
D.   Republican

3) When it was written, the Constitution of the Confederate State of   3. _____
America illustrated that a main philosophical difference between the North and South was the

A.   relationship of states to the national government
B.   impact of party politics
C.   universality of Supreme Court decisions
D.   power of the executive branch

4) The term "slavocracy" was used   4. _____

A.   to refer to the political power of slaveholding states in Congress
B.   by Northerners who resented the dominance of the issue of slavery
over other significant political issues, which received scant attention
C.   by Southerners to refer to the sudden electoral significance of freed
slaves
D.   to refer to the South's total dependence on the institution of slavery

5) By 1870, free blacks comprised about _____ percent of the popula-   5. _____
tion of Washington, D.C.

A.   10
B.   30
C.   50
D.   70

6) Of the terms offered by the Republicans to Southerners in the Com-   6. _____
promise of 1877 in exchange for their recognition of Rutherford B. Hayes as
president, the ones that ultimately took effect included

    I.   the removal of all Federal troops from the former Confederate
          states
    II.   the appointment of at least one Southern Democrat to Hayes'
          cabinet
    III. the construction of another transcontinental railroad using the
          Texas and Pacific in the South
    IV.   legislation that would help industrialize the South

A.   I only
B.   I and II
C.   II and IV
D.   I, II, III and IV

7) *I answer that whenever it becomes necessary, in our growth and prog-*   7. _____
ress to acquire more territory, that I am in favor of it, without reference to the
question of slavery, and when we have acquired it, I will leave the people free
to do as they please, either to make it slave or free territory, as they prefer.

The words above were spoken in 1858 by

A.   Stephen A. Douglas
B.   Charles Sumner
C.   Abraham Lincoln
D.   James Buchanan

8)   David Walker's *Appeal to the Colored Citizens of the World*, published   8. _____
in 1829,

       I.   claimed that indifferent Christian ministers deserved some
                  responsibility for slavery
       II.   called for the immediate abolition of slavery
       III.   urged slaves to kill their masters in order to win freedom
       IV.   was vehemently opposed to recolonization

A.   I only
B.   II only
C.   II and III
D.   I, II, III and IV

9)   The Underground Railroad became much more significant after the   9. _____
enactment of the

A.   Missouri Compromise of 1820
B.   Kansas-Nebraska Act of 1854
C.   Fugitive Slave Act of 1850
D.   Compromise of 1850

10)   One of the primary motivations for Republicans to pass the Fifteenth   10. _____
Amendment was that they

A.   needed black voters in order to hang onto power
B.   wanted to prevent former Confederate officials from voting
C.   wanted to bring discriminatory practices such as poll taxes and literacy
tests to a final end
D.   needed to deter the influence of the Ku Klux Klan over Southern poli-
tics

11)   Abraham Lincoln denounced the _____ on the   11. _____
grounds that it "would amount to a perpetual covenant of war against every
people, tribe, and state owning a foot of land between here and Tierra del
Fuego."

A.   Kansas-Nebraska Act
B.   act of secession
C.   Crittenden Compromise
D.   Compromise of 1850

12) Anti-slavery sentiment was at the root of the formation of the _____   12. _____
_____ Party in 1840.

A. Free Soil
B. Liberty
C. Republican
D. Know-Nothing

13) Direct and indirect results of the American Civil War included   13. _____

I. improved standards of living for industrial workers
II. broader scope of federal power
III. expansion of women's roles and spheres of influence
IV. increased government support for business and farming

A. I and II
B. II only
C. II, III and IV
D. I, II, III and IV

14) The Reconstruction-era Dunning School, a school of thought named   14. _____
after Columbia University professor William Archibald Dunning, contended
that

A. equal treatment for freedmen would naturally occur over time as human beings became more enlightened, but could not be compelled
B. the only tool adequate for insuring and protecting the civil rights of
freedmen was the federal government
C. freedmen were incapable of self-government and had themselves made
segregation necessary
D. slavery had been a grievous sin that could only be atoned for through
the enactment of special privileges for freedmen

15) The original organizer of the Compromise of 1850 was   15. _____

A. William Seward
B. John Crittenden
C. Lewis Cass
D. Henry Clay

16) Lincoln's primary rival for the Republican nomination in 1860 was   16. _____

A. William Seward
B. Salmon P. Chase
C. John Bell
D. Simon Cameron

17) The Personal Liberty Laws passed in northern states throughout the first half of the 19th century were designed to

17. _____

A.   counteract the effects of the Fugitive Slave Law
B.   end the practice of imprisonment for debt
C.   encourage the abolition of slavery
D.   extend the rights of privacy to medical records

18) Each of the following battles was a part of (Grant's) Western Campaign, EXCEPT

18. _____

A.   the Wilderness
B.   Fort Donelson
C.   Shiloh
D.   Perryville

19) The 54th Massachusetts Volunteer Infantry is famous for its Civil War service because it

19. _____

A.   bore much of the responsibility for turning back Pickett's Charge
B.   was one of the only northern regiments to travel south and fight for the Confederacy
C.   one of the first official African-American units in the U.S. armed forces
D.   consisted entirely of unpaid soldiers

20) Once he was made General-in-Chief of the armed forces, Ulysses S. Grant's overall strategy for winning the war was to

20. _____

A.   aggressively attack the seat of the Confederate government in Richmond and let the rest of the Confederacy fall as a result
B.   fight a total war that would permanently destroy the South's ability to fight
C.   start fighting the West and move eastward toward Virginia
D.   slowly starve the South by means of a naval blockade and avoid significant bloodshed

21) The Massachusetts Emigrant Aid Company, later the New England Emigrant Aid Company, was founded in 1854 in order to fight against the extension of slavery to _____ Territory.

21. _____

A.   Kansas
B.   Nebraska
C.   New Mexico
D.   Utah

22) The Wilmot Proviso was endorsed by the _____ Party.   22. _____

      I.   Free Soil
      II.   Democratic
      III.   Republican
      IV.   Know-Nothing

A.   I only
B.   I and III
C.   I, III and IV
D.   II and IV

23) In the Reconstruction-era South, 80 percent of Republican votes were   23. _____
supplied by

A.   freedmen
B.   scalawags
C.   carpetbaggers
D.   Redeemers

24) Booker T. Washington believed that the best way for African Ameri-   24. _____
cans to achieve economic and political rights was to

A.   use the existing U.S. court system
B.   emigrate from the United States and launch new societies elsewhere,
preferably in Africa
C.   expand opportunities for vocational education
D.   launch an armed resistance against the oppressive government

25) *" . . . the descendants of Africans who were imported into this country,*   25. _____
and sold as slaves . . . are not included, and were not intended to be included,
under the word "citizens" in the Constitution, and can therefore claim none
of the rights and privileges which that instrument provides for and secures to
citizens of the United States . . . "

The text above is an excerpt from the

A.   Supreme Court's written opinion in its ruling in *Dred Scott v. Sandford*
B.   Supreme Court's written opinion in its ruling in *Plessy v. Ferguson*
C.   Missouri Compromise of 1820
D.   Kansas-Nebraska Act

KEY (CORRECT ANSWERS)

1. B
2. A
3. A
4. A
5. B

6. B
7. A
8. D
9. C
10. A

11. C
12. B
13. C
14. C
15. D

16. A
17. A
18. A
19. C
20. B

21. A
22. A
23. A
24. C
25. A

TEST 4

Directions: Each question or incomplete statement is followed by several suggested answers or completions. Select the one that BEST answers the question or completes the statement. *PRINT THE LETTER OF THE CORRECT ANSWER IN THE SPACE AT THE RIGHT.*

1)   Abraham Lincoln's fundamental argument against the secession of Southern states was that

1. _____

A.   the U.S. government was a Union of people, and not states.
B.   slavery was cruel and could never be allowed in North America
C.   he had the constitutional responsibility to put down acts of sedition or rebellion
D.   the people of the Southern states had not been allowed to vote on secession

2)   The _____ was a violent attempt by Southern whites to "persuade" white Republicans to join the Democratic Party, leaving the Republican Party as an African-American minority?

2. _____

A.   Amnesty Act of 1872
B.   Compromise of 1877
C.   Poll Patrol of 1874
D.   Mississippi Plan of 1875

3)   In their plan for Reconstruction, Abraham Lincoln and Andrew Johnson focused on

3. _____

A.   Southern states' payment of reparations to the Union
B.   the participation of freed slaves in Southern political life
C.   Southern states' rapid re-entry into the Union
D.   punishment of the South for starting the Civil War

4)   For both sides, the Civil War was financed largely by each of the following means, EXCEPT

4. _____

A.   loans
B.   the sale of gold deposits
C.   taxes
D.   printing paper currency

5)   The event that posed a direct challenge to Stephen A. Douglas's advo-   5. _____
cacy of popular sovereignty was the

A.   Kansas-Nebraska Act
B.   *Dred Scott* decision
C.   1860 presidential election
D.   Freeport Doctrine

6)   The Reconstruction Acts of 1867 provided for   6. _____

    I.   extensive loyalty oaths as a precondition of readmission to the
          Union
    II.   ratification of the Fourteenth Amendment prior to readmission
          to the Union
    III. the registration of black voters
    IV.   the creation of five military districts in the seceded states

A.   I and II
B.   I and IV
C.   I, II and IV
D.   I, II, III and IV

7)   Confederate General Thomas J. Jackson earned the nickname "Stone-   7. _____
wall" at the Battle of

A.   Fredericksburg
B.   Chancellorsville
C.   Mechanicsville
D.   First Bull Run (Manassas)

8)   Ulysses S. Grant's 1868 election to the presidency was   8. _____

A.   achieved through Grant's winning a substantial majority of white voters
B.   effected primarily because of the votes of former slaves
C.   interpreted as a sign that Southern states were ready to accommodate
some of the aims of Reconstruction
D.   an overwhelming popular victory that nevertheless achieved a slim
margin of victory in the Electoral College

9)	In the early stages of the war, large prisoner-of-war camps were not	9. _____
used by either side because

A.	hardly any prisoners were taken
B.	the widespread practice of prisoner exchanges precluded the need for
long-term arrangements
C.	prisoners of war were typically farmed out to rural areas to work as
laborers
D.	it was widely known that such camps were a breeding ground for viru-
lent diseases

10)	Which of the following was NOT a battle of the Peninsula Campaign?	10. _____

A.	Seven Pines
B.	First Bull Run
C.	Yorktown
D.	Hampton Roads

11)	In proclaiming and implementing the Emancipation Proclamation,	11. _____
President Lincoln based his authority on the

A.	constitutional duties of the President of the United States
B.	Commerce Clause of the Constitution
C.	concept of natural law
D.	powers of the Commander-in-Chief of the Army and the Navy

12)	Most accurately, the secessionist movement can be said to have been	12. _____
dominated by

A.	border-state moderates who could not support Lincoln's election
B.	extreme Southern nationalists who hoped to establish a separate plan-
tation society
C.	hill-country white supremacists who feared the entry of blacks into
civil society
D.	Southern moderates who wanted to keep the issue of slavery out of
federal control

13)	Which of the following was a result of the 1860 election?	13. _____

A.	all four major party candidates won electoral votes
B.	John Bell carried two Northern states
C.	Northern votes were split fairly evenly between Lincoln and Douglas
D.	Lincoln won a majority of the popular vote

14)   The Southern hunger for additional slave territory to counteract the
effect of free territorial expansion was illustrated by William Walker's tempo-
rary takeover of the government in   14. _____

A.   Santo Domingo
B.   Sonora
C.   Texas
D.   Nicaragua

15)   After Reconstruction, the "New South" wanted the focus of its econo-   15. _____
my to be

A.   transportation
B.   crops other than cotton
C.   cotton
D.   industry

16)   Which of the following events occurred FIRST?   16. _____

A.   First Reconstruction Act
B.   Wade-David Bill
C.   Ulysses S. Grant's presidential election
D.   Fifteenth Amendment ratified

17)   The U.S. slave population   17. _____

A.   increased dramatically from 1800-1860
B.   declined somewhat after the Compromise of 1820
C.   grew at a relatively modest rate of about 2 or 3 percent a year for much
of the first half of the 19th century
D.   remained relatively stable, as many Southern slaves were able to es-
cape to the North or buy their freedom

18)   One significant result of the Emancipation Proclamation was that   18. _____

A.   several border states seceded from the Union
B.   many Republicans became disillusioned with Lincoln
C.   European nations decided not to support the Confederacy
D.   millions of slaves were freed throughout the South

19)   It is generally true that the institution of slavery in the antebellum   19. _____
South

A.   was the source of constant tension between those who owned slaves
and those who did not
B.   created a strong sense of community responsibility among whites
C.   created an egalitarian society among whites
D.   had the effect of devaluing free labor

20)   The Civil War's "Gettysburg of the West" occurred at _____   20. _____
_____, where Henry Hopkins Sibley's Confederate forces were halted in
their invasion of the West by Union forces under the command of Colonel
Edward Canby.

A.   Bear River
B.   Glorieta Pass
C.   Tucson
D.   Valverde

21)   Dred Scott was a slave who sued for his freedom on the grounds that   21. _____

A.   he was captured after he had already been freed by his master
B.   slavery was unconstitutional
C.   he had offered a fair price to purchase his freedom from his master
D.   he had been a slave in a state where slavery was illegal

22)   In order to decide the fate of slavery in the territories, the Kansas-Ne-   22. _____
braska bill drafted by Stephen A. Douglas applied the same principle as the
one used in the

A.   Wilmot Proviso
B.   Missouri Compromise
C.   Compromise of 1850
D.   Dred Scott decision

23)   The reason that Abraham Lincoln famously suspended the writ of *ha-*   23. _____
beas corpus during the Civil War was that he wanted to

A.   have secessionists tried and convicted before military tribunals
B.   keep Kentucky from seceding from the Union
C.   forestall the Ku Klux Klan's influence in the South
D.   keep a group of Maryland secessionists in jail

24) During Reconstruction, Southern blacks most typically   24. _____

A. worked farms as renters and sharecroppers
B. migrated northward
C. owned and worked small farms
D. worked as urban day laborers

25) The 1860 platform of the Republican Party included   25. _____

       I. the abolition of slavery
       II. protective tariffs
       III. free homesteads
       IV. the construction of a transcontinental railroad

A. I only
B. I, II and IV
C. II, III and IV
D. I, II, III and IV

KEY (CORRECT ANSWERS)

1. A
2. D
3. C
4. D
5. B

6. D
7. D
8. B
9. B
10. B

11. D
12. D
13. A
14. D
15. D

16. B
17. A
18. C
19. D
20. B

21. D
22. C
23. D
24. A
25. C

ANSWER SHEET

TEST NO. _____ PART _____ TITLE OF POSITION _____

PLACE OF EXAMINATION _____ DATE _____

(CITY OR TOWN)   (STATE)

RATING

USE THE SPECIAL PENCIL. MAKE GLOSSY BLACK MARKS.

	A B C D E		A B C D E		A B C D E		A B C D E		A B C D E
1	∷ ∷ ∷ ∷ ∷	26	∷ ∷ ∷ ∷ ∷	51	∷ ∷ ∷ ∷ ∷	76	∷ ∷ ∷ ∷ ∷	101	∷ ∷ ∷ ∷ ∷
2	∷ ∷ ∷ ∷ ∷	27	∷ ∷ ∷ ∷ ∷	52	∷ ∷ ∷ ∷ ∷	77	∷ ∷ ∷ ∷ ∷	102	∷ ∷ ∷ ∷ ∷
3	∷ ∷ ∷ ∷ ∷	28	∷ ∷ ∷ ∷ ∷	53	∷ ∷ ∷ ∷ ∷	78	∷ ∷ ∷ ∷ ∷	103	∷ ∷ ∷ ∷ ∷
4	∷ ∷ ∷ ∷ ∷	29	∷ ∷ ∷ ∷ ∷	54	∷ ∷ ∷ ∷ ∷	79	∷ ∷ ∷ ∷ ∷	104	∷ ∷ ∷ ∷ ∷
5	∷ ∷ ∷ ∷ ∷	30	∷ ∷ ∷ ∷ ∷	55	∷ ∷ ∷ ∷ ∷	80	∷ ∷ ∷ ∷ ∷	105	∷ ∷ ∷ ∷ ∷
6	∷ ∷ ∷ ∷ ∷	31	∷ ∷ ∷ ∷ ∷	56	∷ ∷ ∷ ∷ ∷	81	∷ ∷ ∷ ∷ ∷	106	∷ ∷ ∷ ∷ ∷
7	∷ ∷ ∷ ∷ ∷	32	∷ ∷ ∷ ∷ ∷	57	∷ ∷ ∷ ∷ ∷	82	∷ ∷ ∷ ∷ ∷	107	∷ ∷ ∷ ∷ ∷
8	∷ ∷ ∷ ∷ ∷	33	∷ ∷ ∷ ∷ ∷	58	∷ ∷ ∷ ∷ ∷	83	∷ ∷ ∷ ∷ ∷	108	∷ ∷ ∷ ∷ ∷
9	∷ ∷ ∷ ∷ ∷	34	∷ ∷ ∷ ∷ ∷	59	∷ ∷ ∷ ∷ ∷	84	∷ ∷ ∷ ∷ ∷	109	∷ ∷ ∷ ∷ ∷
10	∷ ∷ ∷ ∷ ∷	35	∷ ∷ ∷ ∷ ∷	60	∷ ∷ ∷ ∷ ∷	85	∷ ∷ ∷ ∷ ∷	110	∷ ∷ ∷ ∷ ∷

Make only ONE mark for each answer. Additional and stray marks may be counted as mistakes. In making corrections, erase errors COMPLETELY.

	A B C D E		A B C D E		A B C D E		A B C D E		A B C D E
11	∷ ∷ ∷ ∷ ∷	36	∷ ∷ ∷ ∷ ∷	61	∷ ∷ ∷ ∷ ∷	86	∷ ∷ ∷ ∷ ∷	111	∷ ∷ ∷ ∷ ∷
12	∷ ∷ ∷ ∷ ∷	37	∷ ∷ ∷ ∷ ∷	62	∷ ∷ ∷ ∷ ∷	87	∷ ∷ ∷ ∷ ∷	112	∷ ∷ ∷ ∷ ∷
13	∷ ∷ ∷ ∷ ∷	38	∷ ∷ ∷ ∷ ∷	63	∷ ∷ ∷ ∷ ∷	88	∷ ∷ ∷ ∷ ∷	113	∷ ∷ ∷ ∷ ∷
14	∷ ∷ ∷ ∷ ∷	39	∷ ∷ ∷ ∷ ∷	64	∷ ∷ ∷ ∷ ∷	89	∷ ∷ ∷ ∷ ∷	114	∷ ∷ ∷ ∷ ∷
15	∷ ∷ ∷ ∷ ∷	40	∷ ∷ ∷ ∷ ∷	65	∷ ∷ ∷ ∷ ∷	90	∷ ∷ ∷ ∷ ∷	115	∷ ∷ ∷ ∷ ∷
16	∷ ∷ ∷ ∷ ∷	41	∷ ∷ ∷ ∷ ∷	66	∷ ∷ ∷ ∷ ∷	91	∷ ∷ ∷ ∷ ∷	116	∷ ∷ ∷ ∷ ∷
17	∷ ∷ ∷ ∷ ∷	42	∷ ∷ ∷ ∷ ∷	67	∷ ∷ ∷ ∷ ∷	92	∷ ∷ ∷ ∷ ∷	117	∷ ∷ ∷ ∷ ∷
18	∷ ∷ ∷ ∷ ∷	43	∷ ∷ ∷ ∷ ∷	68	∷ ∷ ∷ ∷ ∷	93	∷ ∷ ∷ ∷ ∷	118	∷ ∷ ∷ ∷ ∷
19	∷ ∷ ∷ ∷ ∷	44	∷ ∷ ∷ ∷ ∷	69	∷ ∷ ∷ ∷ ∷	94	∷ ∷ ∷ ∷ ∷	119	∷ ∷ ∷ ∷ ∷
20	∷ ∷ ∷ ∷ ∷	45	∷ ∷ ∷ ∷ ∷	70	∷ ∷ ∷ ∷ ∷	95	∷ ∷ ∷ ∷ ∷	120	∷ ∷ ∷ ∷ ∷
21	∷ ∷ ∷ ∷ ∷	46	∷ ∷ ∷ ∷ ∷	71	∷ ∷ ∷ ∷ ∷	96	∷ ∷ ∷ ∷ ∷	121	∷ ∷ ∷ ∷ ∷
22	∷ ∷ ∷ ∷ ∷	47	∷ ∷ ∷ ∷ ∷	72	∷ ∷ ∷ ∷ ∷	97	∷ ∷ ∷ ∷ ∷	122	∷ ∷ ∷ ∷ ∷
23	∷ ∷ ∷ ∷ ∷	48	∷ ∷ ∷ ∷ ∷	73	∷ ∷ ∷ ∷ ∷	98	∷ ∷ ∷ ∷ ∷	123	∷ ∷ ∷ ∷ ∷
24	∷ ∷ ∷ ∷ ∷	49	∷ ∷ ∷ ∷ ∷	74	∷ ∷ ∷ ∷ ∷	99	∷ ∷ ∷ ∷ ∷	124	∷ ∷ ∷ ∷ ∷
25	∷ ∷ ∷ ∷ ∷	50	∷ ∷ ∷ ∷ ∷	75	∷ ∷ ∷ ∷ ∷	100	∷ ∷ ∷ ∷ ∷	125	∷ ∷ ∷ ∷ ∷

ANSWER SHEET

TEST NO. _____ PART _____ TITLE OF POSITION _____

(AS GIVEN IN EXAMINATION ANNOUNCEMENT - INCLUDE OPTION, IF ANY)

PLACE OF EXAMINATION _____ DATE _____

(CITY OR TOWN)   (STATE)

RATING

USE THE SPECIAL PENCIL. MAKE GLOSSY BLACK MARKS.

	A B C D E		A B C D E		A B C D E		A B C D E		A B C D E
1		26		51		76		101	
2		27		52		77		102	
3		28		53		78		103	
4		29		54		79		104	
5		30		55		80		105	
6		31		56		81		106	
7		32		57		82		107	
8		33		58		83		108	
9		34		59		84		109	
10		35		60		85		110	

Make only ONE mark for each answer. Additional and stray marks may be
counted as mistakes. In making corrections, erase errors COMPLETELY.

	A B C D E		A B C D E		A B C D E		A B C D E		A B C D E
11		36		61		86		111	
12		37		62		87		112	
13		38		63		88		113	
14		39		64		89		114	
15		40		65		90		115	
16		41		66		91		116	
17		42		67		92		117	
18		43		68		93		118	
19		44		69		94		119	
20		45		70		95		120	
21		46		71		96		121	
22		47		72		97		122	
23		48		73		98		123	
24		49		74		99		124	
25		50		75		100		125	